GLASGOW ART GALLERY AND MUSEUM
The Building and the Collections

The authors:

Natural History
Geoffrey Hancock, *Keeper*

Archaeology, Ethnography and History
Helen Adamson, *Keeper*
Margaret Buchanan, *Depute Keeper*
Robert Woosnam-Savage, *Assistant Keeper*
Antonia Lovelace, *Assistant Keeper*
Andrew Foxon, *Assistant Keeper*
Julian Jacobs, *former Assistant Keeper*

Decorative Art
Brian Blench, *Keeper*
Rosemary Watt, *former Depute Keeper*
Simon Cottle, *Depute Keeper*
Juliet Kinchin, *former Assistant Keeper*
Jonathon Kinghorn, *Assistant Keeper*

Fine Art
Anne Donald, *Keeper*
Sheenah Smith, *Depute Keeper*
Hugh Stevenson, *Assistant Keeper*
Jonathan Benington, *Assistant Keeper*

Collins and Glasgow Museums and Art Galleries
acknowledge the generous help of

Clydesdale Bank PLC
in the preparation of this book.

G·L·A·S·G·O·W
ART GALLERY AND MUSEUM

With an introduction by Alasdair A. Auld
Director, Glasgow Museums and Art Galleries

COLLINS
London and Glasgow
in association with
Glasgow Museums and Art Galleries

This book illustrates more than 600 of the thousands of objects in Glasgow Art Gallery and Museum in Kelvingrove Park. For reasons of space and conservation requirements, it cannot always be guaranteed that an object illustrated will be on display.

The sizes of the objects are indicated in the captions in *cm* (centimetres) and *in* (inches). Where dimensions are given, the first figure refers to the height of the object and the second to its width.

First published 1987

Published by William Collins Sons and Company Limited

© Glasgow Museums and Art Galleries

ISBN 0 00 435681 0 (Gallery edition)

ISBN 0 00 435682 9 (Collins edition)

© ADAGP 1987   Georges Braque *Still Life*
Charles Camoin *Place de Clichy, Paris*
André Derain *Blackfriars*

© DACS 1987   Emile Bernard *Landscape St Briac*
Henri Matisse *Head of a young girl*
Pablo Picasso *The flower seller*
Paul Signac *Coal crane, Clichy*
Paul Signac *Sunset at Herblay*
Edouard Vuillard *Mother and child*

Design and Art Direction: Sandy Hamilton, Judith Wilder, Alasdair Robertson
Glasgow Museums and Art Galleries Design Department

Photography: E.J. Stewart, Ina Graham, Ellen Howden
Glasgow Museums and Art Galleries Photography Department

Index: Patricia Bascom

Printed in Great Britain by Collins Glasgow

Typeset by John Swain and Son Ltd

Colour origination by Arneg Ltd

Glasgow Museums and Art Galleries Department is grateful to copyright holders for permission to reproduce the following works:

D. Muirhead Bone *The Court of the Lions, Alhambra; Glasgow International Exhibition 1901* (three views)
Francis C.B. Cadell *Interior — the orange blind*
David Y. Cameron *The baths of Caracalla*
Anthony Caro *Table piece Z85 — tiptoe*
Robert Colquhoun *The lock gate*
Alan Davie *Magic picture no. 45*
Joan Eardley *A stormy sea no. 1*
J.D. Fergusson *Damaged destroyer; The pink parasol: Bertha Case*
William Gear *Summer garden*
William G. Gillies *Still life*
W. Goscombe John *The elf*
George Henry *Japanese lady with a fan; A Galloway landscape; The Druids — bringing in the mistletoe*
Robert Houston *Glasgow Art Gallery and Museum — rear view of bronze group*
Ben Johnson *The keeper*
William Johnstone *Border landscape: the Eildon Hills*
Sir John Lavery *Glasgow Exhibition, 1888*
P. Wyndham Lewis *Froanna, the artist's wife*
Laurence S. Lowry *A village square*
Robert MacBryde *The backgammon player*
J. Pittendrigh Macgillivray *Thenew, mother of St Kentigern*
Bruce McLean *Untitled 1984*
Ben Nicholson *Still life 1946-1950*
Eduardo Paolozzi *Hamlet in a Japanese manner*
Anne Redpath *Pinks*
William Roberts *The dancers*
Benno Schotz *Self portrait*
Walter R. Sickert *Sir Hugh Walpole*
Stanley Spencer *The Glen, Port Glasgow 1952*
Graham Sutherland *Flying bomb depot: the caverns, St Leu d'Esserent 14.1.45*
Ossip Zadkine *The music group*

Contents

Introduction

by Alasdair Auld

The history of Glasgow's municipal museums and galleries is a long and interesting one. They were founded in 1854 with a magnificent collection of paintings bequeathed by Archibald McLellan, together with a building to house it. That building, known as the McLellan Galleries, still stands in the busy shopping area of Sauchiehall Street where it is used for meetings and exhibitions. Archibald McLellan (1796-1854), a coach-builder and Deacon-Convener of the Trades House, had been an ardent and discriminating collector from an early age, but there were complications to his bequest as at the time of his death he was insolvent, and the Corporation of Glasgow (as it was then) had to agree to pay his creditors. After some delay this was done, the art collection being purchased for £15,000 and the building for £29,500.

While the city's collection of paintings remained at the McLellan Galleries, in 1870 the Corporation acquired a small mansion called Kelvingrove House about one mile to the west to house objects of a historical and scientific nature. Built in 1783 for Patrick Colquhoun, a former Lord Provost of the city, to a design by Robert Adam, it became known as Kelvingrove Museum. In 1876 a wing was added to display technological items, but it was later decided that a larger building should be built on the Kelvingrove site to bring the city's art and museum collections under one roof. Thus, in 1888, a great international exhibition was held in Kelvingrove Park, beside the house, with the aim of raising money for the new building. The exhibition was a success, and in 1891 a competition was launched by the Association for the Promotion of Art and Music for the design of the new building. According to the original brief, it was also to have included a concert hall and a school of art. The latter plan was dropped, however, and the Glasgow School of Art off Sauchiehall Street was subsequently built to an exciting design by Charles Rennie Mackintosh.

From the 62 plans received as a result of the competition, six were selected for further detailed drawings, and the winners, John W. Simpson and E.J. Milner Allen, chosen by the adjudicator, Sir Alfred Waterhouse, the architect who had designed the Science Museum in London. In 1896, the original promoters of the scheme, the Association for the Promotion of Art and Music, ran out of money, and the project was handed over to Glasgow Corporation for completion. The marble foundation stone, which can be seen today in the North Entrance Hall, was laid on 10 September 1897 by the Duke of York, and the building itself was officially opened on 2 May 1901 by Princess Louise, Duchess of Fife, the City Fathers taking the opportunity to celebrate the event by holding a second international exhibition within the surrounding park.

The 1901 Exhibition ran until 9 November and was a tremendous and popular success. Like that of 1888, it contained a wealth of fine

Muirhead Bone (1876-1953) Glasgow International Exhibition 1901 — entrance to the Industrial Hall from the piazza, *etching.*

Robert Houston (1891-1940) Glasgow Art Gallery and Museum — rear view of bronze group *St Mungo protecting Art and Music* by George Frampton, with Glasgow University beyond, *colour aquatint.*

Harry Spence (1860-1928) Glasgow
International Exhibition 1901 — Restaurant
No. 2 with the Industrial Hall beyond, *oil.*

art as well as historical items and industrial products from all corners
of the world, which were displayed in specially built pavilions reflecting the architecture of the participating countries. One of the principal lenders to the Exhibition was William Burrell (later Sir William),
a town councillor and a member of the organizing committee. Among
the more than two hundred items he lent were numerous paintings, including works by the Maris brothers, Manet, Crawhall and
Daumier, and a large collection of glass, ivories, enamels, carpets
and tapestries. Many of these objects are now on show in the Burrell
Collection in Pollok Park.

The Art Gallery and Museum, Kelvingrove, is an ornate and digni-
fied building and in its day was considered the ideal setting in a great
and important city for the treasures transferred to it at the close of the
1901 Exhibition. These included the collections of fine art, decorative
art, scientific and historical objects, already of a high standard, which
were brought together from the McLellan Galleries and Kelvingrove
House and displayed for the opening to the public of the Art Gallery
and Museum, Kelvingrove, on 25 October 1902.

The building's masonry is externally of red Locharbriggs stone and
internally of white Giffnock stone. The twenty display galleries are
grouped around two side courts and one large centre hall of impressive
proportions. Around the internal courts the names of the various
trades of Glasgow, of famous musicians, poets and artists, and of
Scottish historical characters, are carried on shields and escutcheons.

The opening of the new museum brought the number in Glasgow at
the beginning of the century to six: the Art Gallery and Museum at
Kelvingrove, the People's Palace, and branch museums at Camphill
House, Tollcross House, Mosesfield and Aitkenhead House, and
marked the consolidation within the Corporation of Glasgow of a
department concerned with the proper care and continuation of an

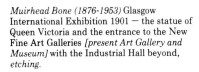

Muirhead Bone (1876-1953) Glasgow International Exhibition 1901 — the statue of Queen Victoria and the entrance to the New Fine Art Galleries *[present Art Gallery and Museum]* with the Industrial Hall beyond, *etching.*

important area of education and interest. The last three have since ceased to function as museums while others have been added to the list (see Branch Museums).

Since the 1850s the Department has had a number of longserving and distinguished Superintendents and, later, Directors. The first Superintendent was James Paton who served from 1876 to 1914 and who masterminded the setting up of the new Art Gallery and Museum but also did so much to set the standards of curatorship which have been followed ever since. His successor, Gilbert A. Ramsay, served for only a short time before enlisting to fight in the First World War. On his death in battle in 1915, Thomas Rennie took over as Acting Superintendent until 1918, to be succeeded by T.C.F. Brotchie who retired in 1930. James Eggleton followed as the first Director and retired in 1938. Dr T.J. Honeyman then became Director, and this period saw great growth in the Fine Art sections with the donation and bequest of some magnificent collections, including Burrell's, as well as the purchase of a number of superb items.

In 1948, the separate posts of Director of Art Gallery and Director of Museums were created, Dr Honeyman continuing as the former while the Directorate of Museums was filled by Dr S.M.K. Henderson. On Dr Honeyman's resignation in 1954, Dr Henderson became Director of both the Museums and the Art Gallery. Although not the publicist that Dr Honeyman had been, he nevertheless succeeded in establishing a rapport with the Corporation and managed to increase the staff. During his time in office, Pollok House and its collection of Spanish paintings came to the Department and the vexed question of where the Burrell Collection should be located was resolved. Dr Henderson retired in 1971 and was succeeded by Trevor A. Walden, who came from the Directorship of Leicester Museums and who greatly augmented the staff and the Museums' budget. It fell to Trevor Walden to oversee the final plans for the housing of the Burrell Collection. Although he saw the start of the work in Pollok Park in 1978, sadly he died in 1979 with little more than the work on the foundations finished. These men and their dedicated staffs did much, often in very difficult circumstances, to make the Museums and Art Galleries Department what it is today, with its headquarters at the Art Gallery and Museum, Kelvingrove, serving nine museums, employing nearly 350 staff, and attracting by 1986 over two and three-quarter million visitors in the year.

Muirhead Bone (1876-1953) Glasgow International Exhibition 1901 — view from the dome of the Industrial Hall, with the River Kelvin and the water chute beyond, *etching.*

At the centre of the Department's work at Kelvingrove are the curatorial departments responsible for the collections of items within the areas of Natural History, Archaeology, History and Ethnography, Decorative Art and Fine Art. Besides being responsible for the display, exhibition and care of the objects in their guardianship, the keepers and their staffs publish the results of their research into the collections. While a tremendous amount of work has already been done in researching the thousands of different objects within the building, with every day that more information comes to hand, new interpretations have to be made so that as accurate a picture as possible can be presented of each item and how it fits into its historical context. Apart from a few, like hallmarked silver or some later 19th-century crafts which have evidence of date and place of manufacture, rarely do pieces have their history attached to them. Most objects, therefore, must be researched in detail before positive statements can be made about them. This curatorial detective work can be laborious and time-consuming, but it is extremely rewarding when new information does come to light.

Susan Crawford (1865-1918) Glasgow International Exhibition 1901 — the Russian pavilions, *etching.*

Preserving our heritage is at the root of the work of the curatorial departments. Over the past twenty years techniques have been developed greatly, and today the main consideration is conservation, not necessarily complete restoration. It is always preferable to conserve a work of art in its present state rather than restore and retouch it in such a way that the process cannot be reversed. Paintings are stabilized and retouched for cosmetic reasons, but these retouches are laminated between coats of varnish which can easily be removed, and other items are similarly treated with reversible processes. Glasgow is fortunate to have qualified conservators in all disciplines, some working in branch museums, others at the headquarters of the Department at the Art Gallery and Museum, Kelvingrove.

As well as conservation, no progressive museum can exist today without the important back-up services of photography, design, and publications. A photographic section has been in existence since 1948, taking photographic records of objects for registration and for publications and publicity. This in turn led in the early 1970s to the setting up of a Design Department, which enabled the work of the whole Museums and Art Galleries Department to be shown in the best possible light.

Publications which are well written, illustrated, designed and printed are good advertisements for the work and purpose of Glasgow's Art Galleries and Museums. Catalogues, books, leaflets and postcards, all give visitors an indication of the size and scope of the collections, making them more meaningful and useful, and they also bring in revenue, as does the licensing of rights to outside bodies to reproduce paintings and objects from the collections. The publications officer is also responsible for all publicity, press views and handouts, and edits the *Calendar of Events,* the quarterly magazine of the Friends — the Glasgow Art Gallery and Museums Association.

In order to offset at least some of the costs of fulfilling a museum's function of preserving our heritage and keeping it secure for everyone, now and in the future, to enjoy, the administrators of museums and galleries today have to be aware of the commercial possibilities these

Maclure and Macdonald, printers Panoramic view of Glasgow International Exhibition 1901, showing, left to right, Concert Hall, Industrial Hall, New Fine Art Galleries *[present Art Gallery and Museum]*, Glasgow University, *colour print.*

institutions can provide. Glasgow is no exception, and the Art Gallery and Museum, Kelvingrove, has a large and flourishing sales organization with a substantial turnover and, even more importantly, profit. Each branch museum also has a sales point, emphasizing its own characteristics and gearing its sales material to its clientele. Much is still being done, and the expansion of such shops is by no means exhausted.

In 1941 the Schools Museum Service was founded with the aim of giving specific education to children either as formal courses of study or as more informal tours. This scheme, which was started with a staff of one, now employs twelve trained teachers from the Education Department of Strathclyde Region and deals with upwards of 100,000 schoolchildren a year. Classes from schools in all parts of Strathclyde learn the fundamentals of art appreciation and an understanding of history and the world around them by access to the museum, its collections and its staff. Courses are also held at the Museum of Transport and at the Burrell Collection, and some classes visit the other branches of the Department. The teachers work in close harmony with the museums' staff and do invaluable work.

In 1944, Dr Honeyman, as Director, set up a friends organization, the Glasgow Art Gallery and Museums Association, or GAGMA as it is more familiarly known. Over the years this has proved to be a great success and has provided the Department with encouragement, financial support and help in a variety of ways, not least of which has been the highly successful system of volunteer guides, who are on hand at several of our museums and art galleries to answer questions about the exhibits and to guide visitors around the collections. The Friends form the basis of our mailing list and are invited to attend exhibition openings and social functions.

The incredible generosity of the many benefactors who have bequeathed or donated objects of all kinds, big and small, valuable and interesting, have made Glasgow's Museums and Art Galleries the great institution it is today. This book will give some indication of the range and depth of our collections in the Kelvingrove building and the dedication of members of staff past and present to make them available to everyone and to demonstrate the excitement that they feel about the objects in their care.

Natural History

Introduction

Natural History is a useful general title for a museum department which embraces three distinct academic disciplines, namely geology, botany, and zoology. Each discipline has its own special methods of collecting and preserving and each needs trained staff. The current volume of knowledge and constant developments in techniques demand such people to cater for the proper management of collections once these reach a certain size.

The three basic elements of geology, botany and zoology come together in those displays which treat the environment as a whole, presenting the fauna and flora according to the habitats which make up landscapes. The structure of a landscape evolves from its underlying rocks and the geological processes to which they are subjected over millions of years. Illustrating these, the Museum collections include pyromorphite [1], a lead mineral which occurs in the mines at Leadhills in Lanarkshire; heulandite [2], a zeolite mineral found in cavities and fissures in Carboniferous age lavas at several localities around Glasgow including the Kilpatrick Hills; and chalcopyrite [3], an important ore of copper, from the lead workings at New Glencrieff Mine, Wanlockhead, Dumfriesshire. A collection of prehnite — a mineral which occurs in igneous rocks — from Boyleston Quarry [4], Barrhead, Renfrewshire, was made by Museum staff in 1972 before the closure of this well-known locality. Good specimens are harder to find now that the quarry is no longer being actively worked.

How a landscape has evolved in turn dictates the pattern of human settlement — the availability of raw materials, the type of soil, the presence of navigable rivers, and so on — making an understanding of geology vital to interpreting the development of towns and cities. Such a basic role as this explains why all well-established museums have had displays and collections of natural history since their beginnings.

Glasgow is no exception to this general rule. The first museum administered by the city was Kelvingrove House, which was purchased in 1870 to house temporarily collections of items in the areas of natural history, archaeology and industrial history. The accessions book, which recorded the gift or purchase of all items, shows that the first few to be acquired included a collection of minerals followed by a selection of shells from a Dr J. Dougal. Other notable gifts which were made during this first year of public museums in Glasgow and which can still be seen today were a Neptune's Cup sponge and

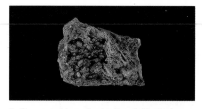

1. *Pyromorphite, a lead mineral. From the collection of Professor John Fleming, donated in 1902 by Major J.A. Fleming, length 6.4cm (2¼in).*

2. *Heulandite, a zeolite mineral, received in 1977, length 13cm (5¼in).*

3. *Chalcopyrite, an important ore of copper found in small quantities in lead workings at Wanlockhead, Dumfriesshire, received in 1976, length 4.7cm (1¾in).*

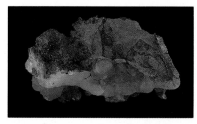

4. *Specimen of prehnite, a mineral occurring in the Carboniferous age lavas of the Glasgow area, length 11.4cm (4½in).*

The osprey, a bird of prey.

5. *The skeleton of a moa, an extinct bird, height 3m (10ft).*

6. *The Geology Room at the Art Gallery and Museum, Kelvingrove, about 1920.*

the skeleton of a moa [5], an extinct ostrich-like bird from New Zealand. The moa is thought to have died out before colonization by western man as only Maori tradition supplies the little information there is on these birds.

Early displays in the Art Gallery and Museum were arranged quite differently from today's, as can be seen in the view of the Geology Room photographed about 1920 [6]. Every object was on show, regardless of its suitability for exhibition. Even microscopic specimens on slides, which could not be distinguished by the unaided eye, were shelved with more visible objects. Microscopic animals and plants are now displayed by using photography and graphic art, or by having appropriate instruments for visitors to view them direct.

If there were several specimens of the same common species, these were given equal prominence with rarities. Where there was not enough room for every item in one display case, then the drawers of the cabinet beneath could be pulled out. Unfortunately, excessive fading resulted from exposing organic material to daylight, and the constant jostling of specimens kept in the drawers led to damage. Current fashion in displays is to show a selection of objects, chosen to illustrate a theme or as examples of particularly attractive or interesting species. In the farmyard case [7], the animals are shown in a naturalistic setting, with domesticated beasts alongside the birds and mammals which have colonized this man-made habitat.

Because no two individuals of any one species are exactly alike, the Natural History department acquires as many examples as possible of each species in which it is interested. These are not regarded as duplicates, although superficially they may seem to be the same. Just as a shepherd can distinguish each of his sheep, the same principle applies for those who study in detail all the huge variety of life forms.

7. *A farmyard habitat on display.*

8. *Brachiopods, two-shelled marine invertebrate animals, among the commonest fossils of the Carboniferous rocks around Glasgow, width of specimen top left 6.7cm (2⅝in).*

Also to be catered for if a collection attempts to be complete are the various stages of development of life forms to maturity, their sexual differences and changes brought about by environmental or geographical variations. There are therefore many more specimens in the department's reference collections than could be displayed or would even be suitable for exhibition in a modern gallery. In this respect, the Natural History collections can be likened to an iceberg. What the visitor sees on display is just the tip, while beneath is the bulk of the collections, acquired over many years. A group of brachiopods [8], fossils from the locally common Carboniferous rocks, illustrate this variety.

The number of individual items in the Natural History department borders on the astronomical. This is partly a reflection of the diversity of life on earth, with approximately two million living and fossil species of plants and animals known at present. The potential number yet to be described can only be estimated, but it is thought that the number of different kinds of insects alone could well exceed this figure. Although Glasgow does not aspire to collect even one example of every living thing, a comprehensive coverage of at least some groups from certain areas is sought. This is why the Museum purchased specimens of tropical butterflies [9], which were formerly in the Saruman Museum in Sussex and were collected by Paul Smart before dispersal in 1982. The general policy is to acquire examples of the major divisions of plants and animals suitable for display, demonstration or comparison. A concentration of effort is made in the areas where the collections are particularly strong. These are outlined under the various headings which discuss the function and methods of the Natural History department.

9. *A drawer of tropical butterflies, recently purchased, pinned and set in a standard way to allow immediate comparison, 40.5 × 40.5cm (16 × 16in).*

Acquisition and Collection

Occasionally, collections of museum quality in the field of natural history are sold on the open market. In the 19th century these were more frequent and the sale of large collections made by amateur naturalists kept several London auction houses in business, but such wholesale collecting of plants or animals is not the main aim of present-day natural historians. It is against the spirit of nature conservation and the laws which are designed to protect the environment. In recent years, however, Glasgow has been able to obtain some good-quality display and reference material by purchase at public auction or from certain suppliers who are aware of our requirements. In 1981, for example, the Museum purchased a partly restored skull of *Mesohippus bairdi* [1], a fossil horse from the Oligocene period of Nebraska in the United States. *Mesohippus* forms a link in the evolutionary line of the horse, which started with *Hyracotherium* about 60 million years ago. Other examples include marine shells of great beauty and display value, as well as collections of land snails which are less imposing to the eye but of scientific interest and most useful for comparison with the local fauna.

Numerically, most specimens received by the department are donated. There are many visitors who bring, as enquiries, specimens which they have found. They are happy to leave the items, be they pieces of rock, plants, or dead animals, in exchange for a definite name and some comment on their natural, or sometimes unnatural, occurrence. The keepers then make the decision on whether or not the objects are of use to the Museum and should be preserved accordingly. As a result of such a specimen being brought in to the Museum in 1938, staff collected at Killearn in Stirlingshire a slab of ripple-marked red sandstone of the Devonian Age [2]. Its 'fossilized' ripple marks are similar to those formed today on the soft bedrock of beaches and river beds by wave or current action.

There are still naturalists who acquire collections during the course of many years' study and who arrange for them to be bequeathed to public institutions. In this way, the material is preserved for future workers in the same field, a useful and satisfying outcome of the time and effort exerted in bringing the collection together.

The opportunity to add significantly to a range of specimens by purchase is limited and the gift of material, although both useful and valuable, has a drawback in that it cannot be predicted or directed. For the Natural History department to build up coherent collections there is no substitute for organized field work. It is necessary, therefore, for the staff to go out and collect material. The sample of *Anthracophausia* [3], a 330-million-year-old shrimp-like crustacean was collected by Museum staff in 1982 from Lower Carboniferous rocks at Manse Burn, Bearsden. Beautifully preserved fossil sharks and other fish, many new to science, were extracted from this now famous locality.

There are constraints to field work. Some animals and plants can be found only at certain times of the year. Regardless of demands

1. *Partly restored skull of* **Mesohippus bairdi,** *a 60 to 70cm-high fossil horse from the Oligocene of Nebraska, U.S.A., purchased 1981, length of skull 19cm (7½in).*

2. *Devonian age red sandstone showing 'fossilized' ripple marks, collected 1938, length 30.5cm (12in).*

3. Anthracophausia *sp., a shrimp-like crustacean from Lower Carboniferous rocks, collected 1982, length 7.5cm (3in).*

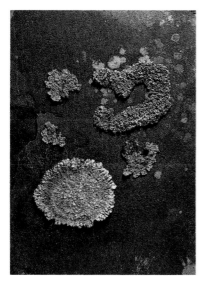

4. *Lichens from the roof of a house in Lanarkshire, diameter of yellow lichen 7.5cm (3in).*

from other quarters, or weather conditions, field work must be undertaken then or not at all. In addition, quite unexpected opportunities can arise, such as when a civil engineering project exposes a new fossiliferous outcrop, demanding immediate action to record and take samples.

Current practice in collecting material ensures that the full circumstances and relevant information are noted. Because this sort of detail is not usually available on specimens in older collections, field work today results in more useful data. Some species of lichens [4], for example, reveal valuable information on the environment as these interesting associations of fungi and algae growing together have a range of sensitivity to air pollution.

The techniques used by the Museum to collect specimens vary according to the species being sought. It would be inefficient to catch fish using a rod and line, but an insect collector's net is still one of the most effective ways of sampling insects. To obtain a complete picture of the fauna of an area, several different methods used together are most successful. In the case of insects, traps with a variety of baits, such as rotting meat, attract carrion-feeding beetles and flies. Light-traps have special bulbs or tubes containing mercury vapour which produces wavelengths of light irresistible to night-flying insects [5]. The apparatus is normally set up and left in a suitable locality overnight, and moths, which form the majority of the catch, settle inside the box. Biting species of insects are often sampled by the simple expedient of baring an area of skin.

When the Natural History department goes on field work, relatively simple techniques can result in large numbers of specimens. Thousands of small shells can be sieved from sand, mites extracted from leaf litter or marine specimens from amongst seaweeds [6]. Collecting and recording by Museum staff on the seashore is continuing a long tradition of marine studies in the Clyde area. For example, David Robertson (1806-1896), who founded the Marine Biological Association at Millport on the island of Cumbrae, made collections which are preserved in the Museum. A few hours' collecting can mean days or weeks of sorting, identifying and cataloguing. Surplus

5. *A light-trap being set up.*

6. *Collecting intertidal marine specimens.*

material can be used for exchange, usually between museums, to obtain species otherwise unavailable in the area.

To be of value for reference purposes, and hence scientifically useful, all the circumstances regarding a specimen have to be noted. As a minimum, each item or sample must be labelled with its place of origin, date of collection, and the name of the collector.

One of the relatively new functions of the department is to record information which is not necessarily directly related to specimens in the collection. These data files ideally describe areas, usually a single site or habitat, in terms of their geographical limits, geological history, and the past and present flora and fauna. The essential factor in organizing data on specimens is that the information is retrievable on request by naturalists, planners, conservationists, or the staff themselves. These are also the people who provide some of the raw data, so that a complete picture of the environment is gradually built up. In this respect, Glasgow has a particular problem in defining the area which the department should cover. Although the information available covers a wide area, the Museum and its Natural History staff are financed solely by the city.

There is one important aspect of field work of which the Museum staff are very conscious. This is the realm of conservation and the legislation which covers the protection of habitats and species. The most relevant of the various acts of parliament is the Wildlife and Countryside Act, 1981. Special licences are needed to acquire or retain certain species, and any holdings must be adequately documented. Plants must not be uprooted except with a landowner's permission. Apart from regulations which cover nature reserves or sites of special scientific interest, some individual species are protected wherever they occur and cannot be disturbed without penalty. Such protection can even preclude photography. Even in deep water conservation is an important factor. The Museum recently obtained examples of solitary and colonial corals [7] from the Hebridean and Porcupine Banks in the North Atlantic, just to the west of the British Isles. These specimens were recovered at depths from 800 to 1,500 metres (2,600 to 4,900 feet) and are from a habitat sensitive to change. Details of the restrictions and recommended codes of conduct are given in various leaflets produced by the Nature Conservancy Council and other bodies, and these can be obtained through the Museum.

Conservation is a relatively new subject, and the Museum has a particular role to play by displaying examples of fossils or recent species of plants and animals which at their natural locations could not be exposed to the pressure of even a small number of visitors. The osprey [8], for example, is a species which has to be protected in Scotland because of pressure by man both directly on the bird itself and on the environment it requires. The same applies to many other kinds of organisms which, because of their shyness, remoteness, or other behavioural traits, cannot normally be seen in the wild. Thus the displays and exhibitions mounted by the department can satisfy normal human curiosity about such rare species as well as illustrate the problems which arise when exploitation of the environment disturbs the delicate balance of nature.

7. *Solitary and colonial corals from British waters, 800 to 1,500 metres (2,600 to 4,900 feet) deep, height of largest cluster 9cm (3¼in).*

8. *The osprey, a bird of prey and now a protected species, length 55.8cm (22in).*

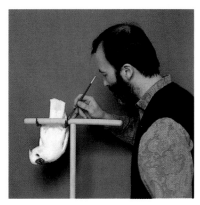

1. *The head and front part of a tiger prepared for display by classic taxidermy techniques.*

2. *A pair of waxwings, traditionally mounted using stuffing materials, wire and glass eyes, height of bird 15.2cm (6in).*

3. *Once mounted in a realistic posture, a cockatoo is retouched.*

Techniques

Taxidermy

Every organism which arrives in the Museum's Natural History department and which is to be kept needs immediate treatment in order to be preserved. In the case of dead birds and mammals, the most pressing problem is to prevent further decay and if they cannot be attended to immediately, they are deep frozen. Other groups are dealt with differently by established methods. Although it is difficult to generalize, there are three basic processes. These are taxidermy, and dry or wet preservation of the whole or part of the organism. Taxidermy is the ability to prepare the skins of animals and to preserve and arrange them in a life-like manner [1]. It can only be done after years of experience and by combining technical and manipulative skills with a knowledge of the behaviour and appearance of animals in the wild. For birds and mammals this traditional method has no substitute, although modern synthetic materials are used for the manikins, or anatomical models, and supporting armatures.

Each specimen is scrutinized in its fresh state and, depending on its condition and the requirements of the department, is treated accordingly. If a certain phase of plumage of a particular bird is unrepresented in the reference collection of skins, then the carcase will be measured and weighed, and the skin removed and preserved for study. Other parts of the body, such as the skeleton and stomach contents, may be kept for reference. In such cases the skin is not given a life-like appearance, as this is both wasteful of storage space and unnecessary for the researching ornithologist. If, however, the species is required for a new display or to replace an old mount, then taxidermy is needed to ensure that the skin is properly preserved and given a realistic posture. The traditional form of mounting birds has a history nearly two hundred years old, and essentially, the same techniques have been used throughout this period. This pair of waxwings, occasional winter visitors to the Glasgow area, are prepared with wires, stuffing materials and glass eyes [2]. Post mortem changes are inevitable although the taxidermist has techniques for making good these defects. For example, once the taxidermist has arranged a bird in the required posture [3], the bill, feet and eyelids have to be painted as these parts lose some colour during drying.

Organic substances on display suffer from fading and can be affected by even the most careful handling. Such damage cannot be rectified. Despite man's ingenuity, he has not been able to make a feather, only birds can. For this reason, the future use of a specimen dictates the method of preservation to be used. Those for reference are preserved according to research needs, with the basic aim of preserving as much of the organism as possible for as long as possible to meet the requirements of scientists in years to come. In some cases the techniques used are traditional; for example, butterflies and moths are pinned and set in such a way that the whole pattern on the wings is visible. The wings are dried while held at right angles to the body to ensure that all the specimens are immediately comparable. Other reference collection specimens, such as the foreign bird species illustrated here [4], are also arranged in a uniform way and labelled adequately to ensure that proper comparison can be made and data easily retrieved.

Some of the recent changes in museum practice can be attributed to new materials and machinery. Freeze-drying, for example, can be used to preserve plants and small animals, whether birds, mammals or invertebrates [5]. It is carried out in a machine which reduces the temperature and pressure to such an extent that water vapour is extracted from specimens without distorting their cellular structure. The three-dimensional form is thus preserved and the internal structure also remains intact.

The changing demands of researchers can result in changes in methods of preservation. The discovery that the soft parts in some groups are more constant and reliable as guides to both species identification and the establishment of higher levels of classification has meant that wet preservation is now more widely used as soft-bodied animals can be satisfactorily kept only in a preservative solution [6], [7]. It used to be normal practice to remove the body from molluscs and keep only the shells. Now, when possible, the whole animal is kept in a solution. Similarly, some insects are no longer dry-pinned but stored in liquids to reduce distortion and make subsequent handling easier.

Even fossils and other geological items need attention following acquisition. Chipping away the matrix which may cover parts of a specimen can be accompanied by chemical treatment. The constituents of many rocks can only be satisfactorily identified by examination under a special microscope [8]. To do this, diamond-tipped saws and grinding machines are used to render slices so thin that they are transparent. The polarizing filters in the microscope then break up the light and the geologist can recognize the characteristic colours of each mineral.

4. Foreign bird species arranged for ease of comparison and reference, length of largest bird 35cm (13¾in).

5. A selection of birds, small mammals, invertebrates and plants preserved by freeze-drying, height of squirrel 12cm (4¾in).

7. Two scorpions (left and right), snake and giant centipede preserved in fluid, height of larger scorpion jar 22.2cm (8¾in).

6. An octopus preserved in alcohol, height 46cm (18in).

8. *A geological microscope being used to identify the mineral constituents of rocks.*

9. *Leatherback turtle cast. They can reach 3m (10ft) in length; this specimen 2.1m (7ft).*

10. *Examples of* Holoptychius, *a Devonian fish, on display with a model reconstruction, length of model 44cm (17¼in).*

11. *The cast of the coelacanth* Latimeria *being made ready for display.*

Display and conservation

There have been marked changes in the last twenty years in the preparation of displays of natural objects, resulting from the adoption or development of new materials and equipment from other, often industrial, applications. The department has a slab [10] which contains several fossil examples of the Devonian period fish, *Holoptychius* sp., and it is displayed with an informative model reconstruction. The slab was donated in 1915 by the British Association who had organized excavations at Dura Den, Fife, to extract specimens from the famous fish-bearing deposits found there.

The use of casting and modelling in resins, foams and cold-setting rubbers is now a regular feature which enables frogs and fish, slugs and sea anemones to be portrayed in a life-like manner. It can also be used on larger animals, such as this leatherback turtle which was cast in resin [9] from an animal found stranded in Luce Bay, near Stairhaven, in September 1975. This method has also been used for the department's coelacanth *Latimeria* which was obtained via the Royal Scottish Museum. From a mould taken from the original fish, the cast was produced and finished [11]. Only after painting in its original colours and the insertion of glass eyes was it ready for display.

Backgrounds to cases can also be produced effectively by using lightweight synthetic materials to create effects almost indistinguishable from the natural environment. The background materials here are a mixture of real materials and cast or modelled ones [12], one of the most difficult features to represent being the surface of water.

The time and manpower spent on preparing specimens for display or reference is considerable. Any factors, therefore, which might cause damage or breakdown have to be controlled. Museum conservation is the prevention or repair of problems which can occur with specimens. Some of these problems can be due to inherent factors in technique, such as the gradual evaporation of liquid preservatives, and there is no substitute in such cases for constant vigilance by museum staff. Other problems can arise suddenly or unpredictably and have to be defined and checked. The identity of a white deposit

12. *A Scottish wetlands habitat reconstructed for display.*

13. *Left, a diseased harp shell; centre, a partly affected cone shell; right, a fresh harp shell; length of cone shell 6.3cm (2¼in).*

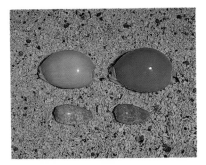

14. *A faded cone shell, bottom left, with a fresh specimen. The golden cowrie, top left, is paler in colour than the other because of geographical variation; length of darker cowrie 9.5cm (3¾in).*

which sometimes forms on shells has been studied recently in the Museum [13], and the conservation scientist has been able to suggest causes and preventative measures. On the left, a harp shell has been affected by the deposit, whereas the right-hand one is a fresh specimen. In the centre, the cone shell has been partly damaged by a particularly large crystalline growth.

Ideally, complete reversal of change should be achieved in conservation, but in practice this can be impossible. Fading, for example, is a well-known threat to displayed objects as the lower pair of cone shells demonstrates [14]. The specimen on the left has been on show for several years. For comparison, the golden cowries at the top have a similar difference in colour but this is natural and due to geographical variation. After a time on display, this kind of difference would become less obvious.

Once an herbarium specimen has been eaten by the dreaded Drugstore Beetle then it cannot be recreated, but despite the fact that the Museum stores are full of items of great delicacy and potential food for hordes of insects, fungi, and bacteria, there are very few problems. This is because of the quality of the initial preparation of specimens, using the best materials, and the careful control of storage conditions under curatorial supervision.

In the department there are some remarkable examples of natural history specimens over two hundred years old and still in good condition. This is testimony to the traditional techniques which are still in use today with slight modifications. Whereas Jamaican rum and Geneva gin were the alcoholic media for fluid preservation in the 19th century, industrial methylated spirits are now used. Arsenic and mercuric compounds have proven efficacy but are now banned by legislation so that chemicals less poisonous to humans are advised for dry specimens. The aim is to have reference collections which are permanent.

Interpretation

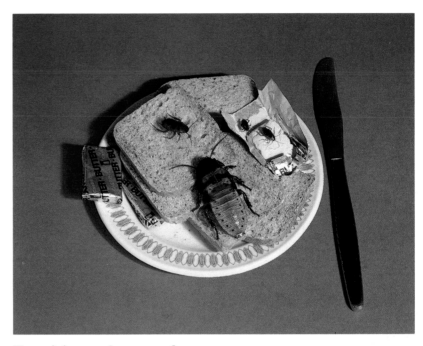

1. *Three species of cockroach, one of which, the largest, is from Madagascar, length 6cm (2⅜in).*

Enquiries and research

Apart from viewing the displays, visitors' most frequent contacts with the Natural History department is in their use of the enquiry service. There are on the staff specialists in the basic disciplines, so the majority of the specimens which are brought in can be identified. Because of the position of Glasgow in world trade, the objects of these enquiries can be of surprisingly cosmopolitan origin. For identifying them, in addition to experience, training and a good library of relevant texts, the most important asset is the reference collection. By comparison with known examples, the mystery of a strange natural object can be resolved to the satisfaction of the enquirer, and it is then often donated to the museum. This can sometimes lead to an unbalanced collection, as in the possibly apocryphal story of a museum with twenty albino moles but no black one.

Enquiries are dealt with from a variety of sources. One of the most satisfying to solve is the identification of a plant or animal which has been a source of concern, such as a pest species of insect or wet-rot fungi, where the true identity of the organism involved is essential to exert control over its population. Cockroaches [1], for example, which are pests in this country are natives of much warmer parts of the world. Many are imported but do not become established. Such, fortunately, is the large tropical cockroach in the middle. The three smaller species are immensely destructive and difficult to eradicate if they become established, so early identification and control is important. In this way the Natural History department has an economic as well as psychological role to play.

Under the general heading of interpretation, that is, the uses to which collections can be put, there are loans, educational use and

research to be considered as well as displays and the provision of an enquiry service. For educational purposes, the Natural History department has a complete skeleton of an ichthyosaur from the Lower Jurassic of Holzmaden in Germany [2]. Ichthyosaurs were marine reptiles and had a shape resembling that of present-day marine mammals such as dolphins and porpoises. This likeness demonstrates the principle of convergence, in which similar characteristics result from the same selective pressures on organisms of different evolutionary origins.

Loans of items are made by the department for many different purposes. Schools benefit from having real objects to examine and discuss in the classroom; artists borrow in order to examine closely the structure and form of natural subjects; scientific loans are made to those who need to compare as many examples of each species as possible to be certain of having a representative sample before publishing their results. Sometimes objects from the Natural History department are used commercially, as props in theatre productions or television advertisements.

On a day-to-day basis, the collections are used mostly by the staff. To have full and accurate documentation of every object is the most basic task. The compilation of such data involves research into the origin, history and identity of each item. This research is particularly important with type specimens like *Hibbertopterus scouleri*, a very rare and important Carboniferous eurypterid sea scorpion [3] from Bathgate, East Lothian. It was discovered by John Scouler in 1831 and became known as 'Scouler's Auld Heid' on account of its resemblance to a human face. A considerable amount of time is

2. Skeleton of an ichthyosaur from the Lower Jurassic of Holzmaden, Germany, purchased 1905, length 2.6m (8ft).

3. Scouler's Auld Heid, Hibbertopterus scouleri, a Carboniferous eurypterid or sea scorpion, donated by Andersonian College in 1902, height 18.5cm (7¼in).

· T I M E B E G A N , I N M I L L I O N S O F Y E A R S ·							
	c.4500	c.570	c.500	c.435	c.395	c.345	c.280	c.225
ERA	Precambrian	Palaeozoic						Mesozoic
PERIOD		Cambrian	Ordovician	Silurian	Devonian	Carboniferous	Permian	Triassic

· T I M E B E G A N , I N M I L L I O N S O F Y E A R S ·								
	c.195	c.135	c.65	c.58	c.36	c.25	c.13	c.2	c.10,000 yrs
ERA			Cenozoic						
PERIOD	Jurassic	Cretaceous	Tertiary					Quaternary	
EPOCH			Palaeocene	Eocene	Oligocene	Miocene	Pliocene	Pleistocene	Holocene

Geological Ages.

4. *Amethyst, a purple variety of the mineral quartz, length 15.5cm (6¼in).*

involved in producing catalogues as the number of specimens in collections of insects, for example, can exceed all other types of museum holdings by several factors.

The need for comparative material when identifying enquiries or field-collected specimens is important. As a result of developing accurate species lists and observations in the field, records of the fauna and flora, past and present, can be made of an area, but specimens must be retained to validate these records. These are necessary preconditions to the production of guides to local habitats and the preparation of displays to illustrate them.

Broader aspects

The natural world provides the raw materials for people to use not only to survive but also to create the less functional cultural trappings. The department can illustrate this basic dependence of mankind on the environment in its displays. Malachite [7], for example, is an important ore of copper, but its attractive appearance has led to its use in jewellery and other ornamental products. Amethyst [4], on the other hand, is a semi-precious stone of purely decorative use whose purple colour results from impurities in the crystal structure of mineral quartz. Sulphur [5], however, cannot be described as anything other than useful. It often occurs near the crater rims of active or extinct volcanoes, where it is deposited by escaping gases.

5. *A specimen of sulphur donated in 1966 by Mr Robert Cochrane, length 16.5cm (6¼in).*

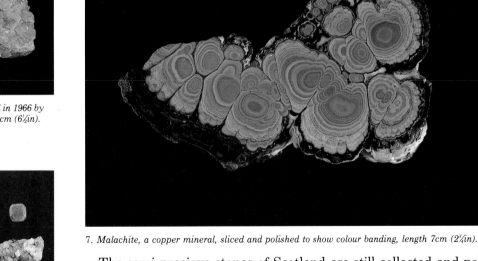

7. *Malachite, a copper mineral, sliced and polished to show colour banding, length 7cm (2¾in).*

6. *Specimens of emerald in its natural rough state, as a cut stone, and set in a gold brooch from the Cunninghame-Graham Collection; height of brooch 6.5cm (2½in).*

The semi-precious stones of Scotland are still collected and polished for use in jewellery, but raw crystalline minerals from other parts of the world have a well-known beauty of their own. Their size, colour and geometry are good enough reasons for display. Emerald [6], for example, is one of the most highly prized of the precious gems. Here it can be seen in its natural state as a rough crystal in its rock matrix and as a cut stone together with a brooch with emeralds set in gold.

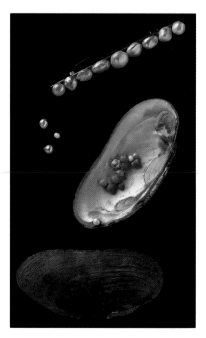

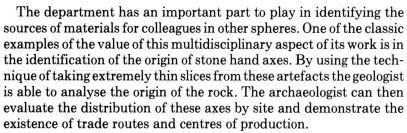

The department has an important part to play in identifying the sources of materials for colleagues in other spheres. One of the classic examples of the value of this multidisciplinary aspect of its work is in the identification of the origin of stone hand axes. By using the technique of taking extremely thin slices from these artefacts the geologist is able to analyse the origin of the rock. The archaeologist can then evaluate the distribution of these axes by site and demonstrate the existence of trade routes and centres of production.

That geology is basic to human evolution is shown in the very names given to the development of our civilization: stone, bronze and iron ages — all materials from the earth's crust. Scotland has an extremely rich and complex geological history. The minerals to be found here and the ores which have been extracted for processing are many and varied. The element strontium, for example, is named after the village of Strontian, near Loch Sunart in Highland Region and was first isolated in 1791 from specimens of strontianite [10], a rare mineral, gathered from this locality. The mines in this area also yield marketable quantities of barytes, galena and blende. Silver has been extracted from various sites in Scotland in sufficient quantities to be made into decorative art objects, such as the goblet [8] made of Scottish silver from Islay, recovered from mines which were working galena, a lead ore. The galena specimen beside it is from Wanlockhead in Dumfriesshire.

Freshwater mussel pearls come from the mussel known as *Margaritifera margaritifera,* seen here [9] with a brooch of pearls from the River Tay in Perthshire. It is the rarity of these pearls as much as their intrinsic attractiveness which has led many people to search for them. Unfortunately, although they occur only in larger, older shells, molluscs of all sizes are being picked out of rivers in large quantities, with the resulting danger that these mussels, like many other living things, may be rendered extinct because of exploitation.

8. Goblet of Scottish silver (c.1780) by the Glasgow silversmith, Adam Graham, purchased 1981, and galena specimen from Wanlockhead, height of goblet 17.5cm (7in).

9. Shell and pearls of the freshwater pearl mussel Margaritifera margaritifera, *widely distributed throughout Scotland, with a brooch of c.1890 containing freshwater pearls, part of the Hull Grundy Gift of jewellery; length of brooch 12cm (4¾in).*

10. A specimen of strontianite from which the element strontium was first isolated in 1791 by Dr Hope of Glasgow University, from the David Glen Collection, length 7.5cm (3in).

11. *The long-tailed field mouse found on St Kilda, with a British mainland specimen, length of St Kilda mouse 17.2cm (6¾in).*

Reference collections

The Natural History department's collections are arranged taxonomically, that is, the specimens are ordered by what are currently understood to be their natural affinities. These relationships are established by research in museums and universities throughout the world, but amateur workers also contribute to developments in this field and are a significant proportion of the users of the collections.

Taxonomy, the theory and practice of classifying organisms, although traditionally associated with the work of museums, is only a small part of the duties of keepers, much of whose time is spent making the collections available to others. Systematists, those who study the diversity of organisms and the relationships between them, use reference collection specimens for research. The variation within species is often very marked and can be best understood when examples from the whole range are brought together. The long-tailed field mouse on St Kilda [11], for example, is larger than the mainland field mouse and has browner stomach fur. These differences are the result of geographical isolation as the St Kilda populations have existed separately from Scottish mainland species, possibly for as much as 10,000 years, when the ice from the last glaciation melted. Present-day plant and animal populations have evolved from earlier forms, and the fossils of related species can give clues to ancestry. *Erretopterus bilobus* [12] is a eurypterid sea scorpion fossil, from the Silurian rocks of Logan Water, Lesmahagow, related to the spider group of animals.

To study the complex interdependence of life on the planet, ecologists rely on the accurate identification of each species involved, otherwise valid conclusions cannot be made. Students of animal behaviour must also be certain exactly which species is being studied. For these reasons, the specimens in the Museum are constantly referred to by a variety of workers in different fields of study.

In order to determine what is understood to be a species, the taxonomist gives each one a scientific name. This is in two parts, a first generic name, for example *Homo*, and a second specific part, say, *sapiens*. Both together are a unique combination, in this case the human species, *Homo sapiens*, literally 'wise man'. This system was

12. Erretopterus bilobus, *a eurypterid, or sea scorpion, of the Silurian period, from the Slimon Collection donated by his family in 1909, height 12.5cm (5in).*

established by a Swedish naturalist, Linnaeus, in the mid-18th century, and he used classical Latin and Greek because they were the languages then universally understood throughout the civilized world. As, up to the present day, so many organisms have had to be described words are now used from various languages. To conform with the earlier usage, however, they are still latinized and are just as descriptive and comprehensible to scientists from different countries. Normally, an example of each newly discovered species is selected and serves as the type specimen. International agreement recommends that type specimens should be deposited in public institutions, usually museums, so that they are available for study by anyone. By common consent they are the property of science and not of individual researchers. They constitute the single most important category of material in natural history museums, often being referred to as the 'building blocks' of biology and palaeontology. The importance of type specimens is that they are the physical evidence of a name given to a species by a taxonomist. Any argument as to which species is meant by a name can be settled objectively by examining the type specimen.

On a more local level, the Museum's function as a repository for voucher material is important. The existence of a plant, animal or fossil at a particular time in a particular place is proved by a voucher specimen in a local collection. The Museum has a large herbarium [13] which was collected by Robert MacKechnie (1902-1978), and which contains many examples of local plants which can be referred to for checking his records.

Such specimens can provide answers to questions which may arise if a record is disputed. They are now also used, for the whole of the British Isles, in mapping schemes to show the distribution of several groups of plants and animals. Where species for the schemes are difficult to identify, records will only be accepted if they are backed up by a specimen deposited in a museum. There are many instances when representative collections of voucher specimens can be made in advance of the destruction of a site. This is particularly relevant when excavations expose rock, and there are obvious parallels here with rescue archaeology. Such a specimen is *Lepidostrobus* [14], a cone belonging to a group of primitive plants called 'scale trees', which flourished during the Carboniferous period. This fossil was found at the Glenbuck opencast coal workings near Muirkirk in Lanarkshire. The opportunity to examine these rocks might not ever recur.

The research uses to which the collections can be put are virtually limitless. New techniques and discoveries mean that new applications are possible, and our close links with Glasgow's universities ensure that these opportunities are maximized. For example, continuing concern about the build-up of pollutants in the environment engenders research. The existence in the Museum of specimens acquired before pollutants such as pesticides were developed allows comparison to be made with modern material. The department also helps to monitor the environment because all the relevant specimens, mainly birds of prey, brought into the Museum are tested for concentrations of poisonous substances.

13. *Consulting the herbarium in which various collections are incorporated.*

14. Lepidostrobus *fossil cone of the Carboniferous period, donated 1981 by Mark Ferrie, length 9cm (3¼in).*

Historical Collections

The result of having acquired material over a long period is that the collections in themselves begin to have their own intrinsic historical value. In some cases, the fact that they were collected by a famous person gives them an added interest. Such a collection at Glasgow consists of specimens brought from Africa by David Livingstone (1813-1873), the explorer and missionary who was also known as a naturalist.

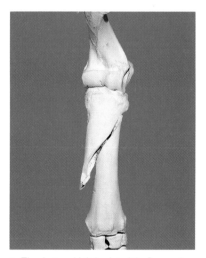

1. *Unsigned portrait of the Clydesdale horse, Baron of Buchlyvie, foaled 16 May 1900, died 30 June 1914.*

Those items which are instantly recognizable as having a place in everyday life or in a local culture are especially interesting. An example of this kind is the skeleton of a horse, the Baron of Buchlyvie. Associated with the skeleton is archival material concerning its breed, the Clydesdale, including the A. Brown photographic collection of Clydesdale horses. Brown was a professional photographer at Lanark who between 1900 and 1959 attended the majority of shows in the West of Scotland where Clydesdales were shown. On the closure of his premises, the entire collection of over four hundred glass negatives was transferred to the Museum. These provide a unique pictorial record of the principal Clydesdale horses over a period of sixty years and complement the Baron of Buchlyvie memorabilia.

The Baron of Buchlyvie [1] was bred in 1900 by Mr McKeoch at Woodend Farm, Buchlyvie in Stirlingshire, and sold at Aberdeen as a two-year-old to Mr James Kilpatrick of Craigie Mains, Kilmarnock in Ayrshire. He won numerous first prizes at major shows. Kilpatrick sold a half share in the Baron to Mr William Dunlop, who offered £2,000 for sole ownership. The offer was accepted and the horse transferred to Dunure Mains, but Dunlop argued that since he already owned half, then the difference due to Kilpatrick was £1,000. An ensuing lawsuit resulted in the Baron being put up for public auction in 1911 and Dunlop purchasing the horse outright for the enormous sum of £9,500, a record for the time. Unfortunately, two years later the Baron broke his left foreleg and had to be destroyed. He was buried in the rose garden at Dunure Mains, but four years later his remains were exhumed and his skeleton was subsequently presented to the Museum [2].

2. *The shattered left foreleg of the Baron of Buchlyvie.*

Natural objects appear regularly in folklore and superstition. In the past, the mystery surrounding often commonly found objects was more easily explained by turning to the supernatural, which seems to have been regularly used to account for fossil remains. Devil's Toe Nails, actually *Gryphaea*, a kind of oyster found in Jurassic deposits, were known as such because of their shape. The pointed, dart-shaped fossil skeletons of belemnites, extinct squid-like animals, were believed to be the earthly manifestations of heavenly anger flung down from the skies during thunderstorms and hence called Thunderbolts. A related group of molluscs, the ammonites, were generally called Snakestones. These coiled shells occur mainly in the bands of Jurassic rocks which run diagonally across the British Isles from the area around Whitby in north Yorkshire to the Dorset coast near Lyme Regis. Snakestones form part of the coat-of-arms of Whitby, and the legend was perpetuated by locals carving fanciful heads on the fossils [3].

3. *Jurassic period fossil of an ammonite found in the 19th century and carved to resemble a snake, width 31cm (12¼in).*

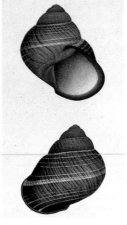

4. *Plate 21 from* Icones Conchyliorum terrestrium*: the Philippine land snail (Helix sarcinosa Broderip), height of top illustration 6.3cm (2⅖in).*

5. *Plate 27 from* Icones Conchyliorum terrestrium: Helix turbinoides *Broderip, height of top illustration 7.5cm (3in).*

6. *Plate 25 from* Icones Conchyliorum terrestrium: Helix polychroa *Sowerby from the Philippines, together with an undescribed species which Gray refers to by the name* Helix tuberculifera *(locality unknown), height of top illustration 4.5cm (1⅞in).*

In the 19th century the public imagination was caught by the strange animals being brought back from abroad by explorers. This interest was exploited by showmen who would put on display and advertise all sorts of creatures. A handbill of 1853 [7] from the Adam White archive collection advertises the display of a Great Anteater, a native of South America, which was put on public exhibition in Broad Street, St Giles, London.

Under the general heading of archives come drawings and manuscript material such as letters, notebooks, diaries and annotations to printed books. These are an important element of collections, sometimes providing the key to understanding them. This is well demonstrated in cases where organisms were illustrated at the time of their discovery. When these illustrations are reproduced in a published book, the specimens are known as 'figured', and in some cases this can establish beyond doubt which are the type specimens for a species. To accompany its holding of land snails and their shells collected by Thomas Gray, the Museum has a copy of his book *Icones Conchyliorum terrestrium* which was published in 1848 and which contains 164 plates of original watercolour drawings and 600 figures illustrating over 400 specimens. Many of the drawings were taken directly from the shells in his collection [4], [5], [6].

By using such a combination of sources, an expert can sometimes distinguish between individual shells of the same species and demonstrate those which in particular are illustrated. Such decisions are made considerably easier if the species is rare or comes from a part of the world only just being explored by naturalists at the time of discovery. *Icones Conchyliorum terrestrium* also includes an illustration of *Pleiodon ovatus* [8], a rare freshwater mussel, thought to be from Liberia in West Africa. None of these shells has been collected since about 1850, and it now may be extinct.

Many important collections, by naturalists such as Charles Darwin, have been divided, distributed or split by auction sale among many institutions. Specimens from the *Challenger's* oceanographic exploration cruise, which lasted four years from 1872, can be found in virtually any museum of note in the country, and Glasgow has its share. This means that good documentation, accurate cataloguing, and good communications with other institutions, as well as a

7. *Handbill featuring the Great Anteater put on public exhibition in London in 1853.*

8. *A specimen of* Pleiodon ovatus, *now possibly extinct, width 10cm (4in).*

9. *Late 18th-century illustration of the Pacific volute shell, annotated by George Humphrey, the leading conchological dealer of the time, length of top illustration 10cm (4in).*

10. *Dr William Hunter's specimen of* Voluta pacifica *in the Hunterian Museum of the University of Glasgow, length 11cm (4¼in).*

11. *Watercolour drawing on paper watermarked 1827 of two swimming crabs and a cake urchin, inscribed 'China, Mr Reeves'.*

sense of the historical importance of collections, are extremely important. Where records are not kept, such collections can end up in different places, their full history and potential unrealized. The unravelling of these chequered histories is a time-consuming but exciting form of detective work which keepers need to pursue. In the case of specimens obtained on Captain Cook's first voyage of exploration, from 1768 to 1771, co-operation with the Hunterian collections at the University of Glasgow has enabled valuable data to be built up. The Museum has an 18th-century illustration of the Pacific volute shell thought to be one of the few shells brought back from Cook's voyage. The illustration [9] has been annotated by George Humphrey, the leading conchological dealer of that time: '*Voluta pacifica* done from that in Dr Wm Hunters Museum/Reef opposite Endeavour River New Holland'. The actual specimen of *Voluta pacifica* [10], obtained by Sydney Parkinson (1745-1771) on the voyage, which eventually passed to Dr William Hunter (1718-1783), is now in the Hunterian Museum.

Archives can also have an aesthetic value. Some collections of archive material are kept in the Natural History department because of their link with famous naturalists. Whereas Thomas Gray's illustrations relate to actual shells, drawings brought back from China in the middle of the 19th century by John Reeves (1774-1856), an Inspector of Tea at the East India Company's establishment at Canton, were not accompanied by specimens [11], [12], but this is not a particular drawback because the colours in the drawings are so accurate and obviously drawn from life that the various species of marine life can be identified. More interestingly, they are superb examples of non-stylized Chinese art from this period, executed by local artists.

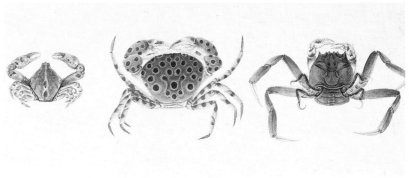

12. *Drawing of three crabs.*

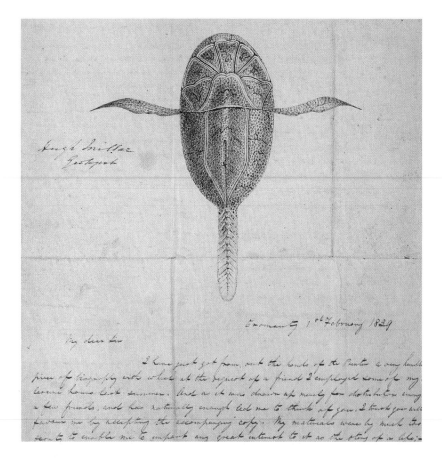

14. *Atkins' cyanotype (c.1847) of the common red-brown seaweed* Ptilota sericea, *height 20cm (8in).*

13. *Front page of a letter written by Hugh Miller in 1839.*

Another important archive piece is a letter [13] written by Hugh Miller (1802-1856) on 1 February 1839 to Professor John Fleming (1785-1857). Such material gives us an insight into a correspondent's thinking at the time, and allows us a glimpse of the concerns, attitudes and development of contemporary scientific thought. In this case, Miller, famous as an author and self-taught geologist, is discussing amongst other things the reconstruction of fossil fish and in his illustration making the first attempt to reconstruct the appearance in life of a fossil fish of the Scottish Old Red Sandstone. These primitive vertebrates are principally of the Devonian Age (c. 300 million years ago) and are one of Scotland's specialities from the Old Red Sandstone period. Their discovery and early recognition were in no small part due to Hugh Miller's ability as a collector and communicator.

Miller says in his letter that

'for some time past I have been amusing myself in figuring this highly curious fossil, and on the first page you have the result of my studies. I am aware my skill may well be doubted; but I have broken up several hundred nodules containing remains of the creature and examined them carefully and as I am unwilling that my observations should be wholly without fruit, I have taken this way of registering them. Like the phrenologists too, who divide their little provinces of brain into the established and merely probable (though I would be sorry if my certainty were not a little more certain than theirs) I have carefully marked those parts

15. *Atkins' cyanotype of 1843 of the brown seaweed* Cystoseira fibrosa *from Part 2 of Volume 1 of* British Algae - Cyanotype Impressions, *height 26cm (10¼in).*

16. *Atkins' cyanotype of 1843 of the red seaweed* Delesseria alata *from Part 5 of Volume 1, height 13.3cm (5¼in).*

17. *A 19th-century dried specimen of the red seaweed* Delesseria alata, *height 12cm (4¾in).*

of the animal of whose shape and position I am assured from those regarding which I am in more doubt; and the former may serve as a sort of halfway stage to future enquiries.'

This, the earliest attempt, actually combined the remains of two different fish into one whole. The front part is of one called *Pterichthys milleri* (named after him by Louis Agassiz, the great fish expert of the day) whereas the tail is of another, called *Coccosteus.* By the time Miller published his most famous work, *The Old Red Sandstone, or New Walks in an Old Field,* in 1841, he had realized this and correctly allocated the relevant front and back ends. Fossils of this kind are rarely found whole and unbroken, so an error such as this is readily understandable.

Another interesting set of works on paper in the Natural History department has implications not just for botany but for the history of science too. This is the work entitled *British Algae — Cyanotype Impressions* by Anna Atkins. It was issued in parts, starting in October 1843, and illustrated seaweeds by using an early photographic technique, known more familiarly today as the blueprint. It is essentially a silhouette made by laying the objects to be reproduced on specially prepared photographic paper and exposing them to strong light. Because it is an exact copy of the specimen's shape and outline, each seaweed is accurately illustrated and in most cases identifiable to the species level. *Ptilota sericea* [14], a common red-brown seaweed which occurs on vertical rocks between tide-marks all around the British coast, *Cystoseira fibrosa* [15], a brown seaweed which occurs below low-water-mark in southwest England and Ireland, and *Delesseria alata* [16], a red species widely distributed around our shores at depths from 18 to 45 metres (24 to 60 feet) are taken from this book. For historical comparison, the Museum also has a dried specimen of *Delesseria alata* [17] from Ayrshire, mounted by David Landsborough or his daughter in 1848. This was sold in a book, *Treasures of the Deep,* to raise funds for the church at Saltcoats.

The Atkins book was not only the first to be produced photographically, but it predates the efforts of more famous names in this sphere, such as Fox Talbot. The copy of Anna Atkins' work in Glasgow is one of only about half a dozen known to exist and is the most complete. It is part of the collections amassed by Adam White, a Scottish zoologist who at the age of nineteen in 1835 was hired to work as assistant keeper of zoology at the British Museum by John George Children, Anna Atkins' father. After suffering a mental breakdown in 1863, White returned to Scotland where he died in a Glasgow asylum in 1879. The Museum was given several of his archives in 1931 by a descendant.

Many other historically interesting specimens and archives are preserved in the department. Some of these are fully researched and are well known to both visitors to the displays and to the scientific community. Others can only be suspected, for it is only when an enquiry is made in a certain area that an investigation can reveal a chain of circumstances, often of great complexity. The end result is that the existing collections grow in basic value as their potential is more fully appreciated, as well as growing in size by being increased by regular acquisitions.

Extinct and endangered species

The Museum houses specimens of several plants and animals which have become extinct for various reasons and at various times, thus providing us with our only information on these vanished species. To gauge the huge size of the Giant Irish Deer *Megaceros giganteus* [18], for example, which died out after the end of the Ice Age 10,000 years ago, we must study the antlers, part of a complete skeleton found at Naul in Ireland, with their spread of 2.75 metres. More recently, in 1805, alpine cotton grass became extinct in Britain. This specimen [19] from the John Fleming herbarium, was collected by Dr Patrick Neill in 1796 before the plant's last site in the Moss of Restenneth, near Forfar, was drained.

There are also specimens of species which are very rare or under

18. *Skull and antlers of the Giant Irish Deer,* Megaceros giganteus, *purchased 1892, width of antlers 2.75m (9 ft).*

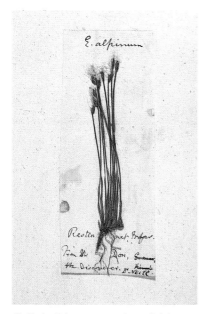

19. *Early 19th-century specimen of alpine cotton grass, now extinct in Britain, height 10cm (4in).*

threat in their natural habitats. These are nearly extinct or endangered mainly as a result of human activity, either deliberate or as a by-product of progress, the latter being well demonstrated by the demise of the unique British race of the large copper butterfly, following drainage of its fens habitat for agricultural improvement. And on the other side of the world, in Sumatra and Borneo the orang-utan [20], a large man-like ape whose name comes from the Malay for 'man of the woods', is currently regarded as being in danger of extinction because of the threat of destruction by man of its preferred habitat in low-lying forests.

Bears and wolves have become extinct in much of Europe because they were in competition with man and a danger to him and his stock. Other unfortunate creatures have pelts or feathers which make them attractive to the fashion trade; ostriches, birds of paradise and the spotted cats are just some of the species threatened by this whim of the western world. Such is the concern for these species which are exploited mainly for their appearance that in many countries laws have been brought into effect to help counteract the threat. The international effort is co-ordinated by the Convention on International Trade in Endangered Species (CITES). In this country such activities are controlled mainly by the Endangered Species (Import and Export) Act 1976, one result of which is that Customs and Excise officers are empowered to seize imported goods made from protected species. Confiscated items can be whole animals or parts of animals used in clothes or ornaments [21]. They are usually destroyed after seizure but sometimes, if suitable, are offered to museums which could not otherwise legally obtain them as a licence to collect would not be granted, even to a museum. Such items are used for study but

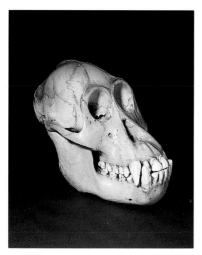

20. *Skull of an orang-utan, a primate currently regarded as being in danger of extinction, height 16cm (6¼in).*

21. *Animal remains and products confiscated by Customs and Excise as their use is in contravention of international law, length of crocodile skin 69cm (27¼in).*

22. *A male huia, extinct since 1907, purchased in 1980, height 33cm (13in).*

also provide display material for the subject of protected animals. In return, the Museum assists Customs and Excise officers by helping to identify some imported items.

By whatever means extinct or endangered organisms arrive at the Museum, their preservation means that researchers can study them. In the case of endangered species, the need to collect more from the wild is reduced. The Museum has, however, in its collections some animal species which are now extinct but which, at the time they were obtained, were quite common. In the 19th century, the North Island of New Zealand was the home of the huia [22], the male of which had a long bill to hook wood-boring insects out of rotting wood. Since 1907, however, the huia has not been seen and must be presumed to be extinct.

Clearly, the provision of such information contributes to the future protection and conservation of other species. To assist in identifying those at risk, *Red Data* books are published at regular intervals by the International Union for the Conservation of Nature. These detail the animals and plants under threat according to their classification and status. As new editions bring the situation up to date, some may change status for the better as a result of successful conservation measures while the names of others are removed as they reach the irrevocable state of extinction. Quetzals [23], revered by the Aztec people and regarded as one of the world's most beautiful birds, have been listed in *Red Data* books since their inception in 1966. It was the relentless pursuit of the male bird for their tail feathers for use in

23. *Pair of male quetzals, from Central America, now endangered, length including tail 53.5cm (21in).*

24. *Shell of the Galapagos rift limpet,* Neomphalus fretterae, *with a related but coiled fossil specimen, width of* Neomphalus 2.1cm (⅞in).

fashion garments, coupled with the destruction of their natural habitat in Central America, which has brought them so close to extinction.

On a happier note, there are occasions when organisms are discovered alive which have hitherto been known only as fossils. The coelacanth fish is now well known as belonging to a group which was thought to have become extinct millions of years ago, until a living descendant was caught off the Madagascan coast in 1938. Live coelacanths are rarely found, and Glasgow has only casts of an adult and of recently discovered embryos (see page 19). The collections do, however, contain an actual specimen of the Galapagos rift limpet *Neomphalus fretterae* [24] which was previously known only from shell fossils. The first living examples of these rare creatures were found in 1952 in deep water off the coast of California. With this exceptional kind of discovery comes the opportunity to examine the anatomy of the soft parts of the body which are not preserved in the fossil state, so helping us to add to our knowledge of evolutionary affinities and biological functions.

The crucial point remains that it is only museums which can provide the experience to a visitor of seeing and examining real objects in detail and at leisure. This is what uniquely distinguishes museums from other institutions concerned with widening our knowledge of the world of which we are part.

Archaeology, Ethnography and History

Introduction

Following the Public Libraries (Scotland) Act of 1867, which identified the local authorities eligible to provide libraries and museums in Scotland, an increasing number of municipal museums were set up. Glasgow was in the vanguard of the movement, the first objects being collected and registered early in 1870.

The first home for these collections was Kelvingrove House, built c.1783 for Patrick Colquhoun, merchant and Provost of Glasgow. It was he who gave the name Kelvingrove to the house and the surrounding land owned by him, the name now preserved in the parkland around the present Museum. The house was demolished in 1899 to make way for the 1901 International Exhibition, but a wing which had been added in 1876 to house objects of technological interest continued to be used and accommodated the Japanese Section of the 1901 Exhibition and the Prehistoric Section of the Historic Exhibition in 1911.

Part of the Department's collections seem to have been displayed in Kelvingrove House, cheek by jowl with Natural History objects, but photographs indicate that the ceramics from Cyprus and Southern Italy were displayed with the paintings in the Fine Art Galleries in Sauchiehall Street, now known as the McLellan Galleries [1].

1. *Interior of the McLellan Galleries in the 1890s.*

Collecting Phases

Although the Department cannot lay claim to the first entry in the Museum register, that honour falls to Natural History, it does claim the second, 'March, 1870, two Japanese swords, presented by Mr Young'. An examination of the entries relating to the Department indicates a general trend of slow but steady growth between the period roughly 1870 to 1890. Many were donations of individual objects or small collections ranging from '1873, urn, Kilmacolm' to 'Russian infantry sword found in the Crimea'.

From about 1872 the entries read increasingly: 'specimens illustrating the manufacture of . . .', anything from tin to textile fabrics, Canadian woods etc. This was very much in keeping with the Department's title in the Museum register, 'The Industrial Museum — Kelvingrove Park', and follows the trend of many museums of the period in displaying manufacturing and craft processes and design from

Gothic Milanese field armour, Italian.

both at home and abroad to educate the public. The collections of the Scottish History section of the Department at the time reflect the emphasis on manufacturing techniques, ranging from examples of straw plaiting from Orkney, to tartans and dyes presented by the Scottish Home Industries Association, and local pottery from the Hebrides.

It is surprising to discover how many objects were being collected from the Western Isles of Scotland between 1870 and 1900, either by people who lived in the Highlands and Islands or by visiting Glaswegians. Objects were being collected from far-flung island groups — St Kilda, North Uist, Harris and Foula. It was not until the 1940s and 50s that these were supplemented with collections of domestic items from Orkney and agricultural and textile-associated objects donated by Messrs William Gowans, Woollen Warehousemen of Glasgow, a firm which dealt with workers throughout the Highlands and Islands.

In ethnography, also, there was an emphasis on manufacturing and craftwork with the acquisition in 1878 from the Japanese Government of a large collection of Japanese domestic items, pottery, textiles and natural products.

From 1890 onwards there is evidence of a change of collecting policy in that there was an increasing tendency to acquire objects and collections by purchase. Presumably this was in response to the fact that in 1891 a competition was launched, by the Association for the Promotion of Arts and Music, for the design of a new, and larger, Museum building, the foundation stone of which was laid on 10 September 1897.

In the field of archaeology the Museum began subscribing to the Egypt Exploration Fund in 1892 and, up to the beginning of World War I, it received a proportion of the finds from each season's excavations, building up an interesting range of Egyptian artefacts. Even in Scottish archaeology purchases were being made. In an Edinburgh saleroom in November 1892 the Museum bought part of the collection of John Rae of Aberdeen, acquiring many objects from Aberdeenshire. Over the following four years flint tools and pottery from Denmark, Sweden, Switzerland, France and Ireland were bought from an Edinburgh collector.

In arms and armour, the first major purchase was made as late as 1911, when the Parsons collection of edged weapons was bought. Sporadic individual donations continued over the years, but in 1939 came the magnificent bequest of Robert Lyons Scott, Chairman of the Scott Shipbuilding and Engineering Company of Greenock [2]. This collection of over 800 items consists in the main of European armour, weapons and books. This was followed closely by another bequest, that of Charles E. Whitelaw, largely composed of Scottish weapons. These two collections were complemented in 1956 by the purchase of the Martin collection of firearms.

The Department has now been acquiring objects for over one hundred years, and in that time has built up wide-ranging collections, some of international importance, others of national or local interest. In the main, the policy now is to supplement and complement existing collections.

2. Portrait of Robert Lyons Scott (1871-1939) by Thomas C. Dugdale R.A. (1880-1952).

Collectors and collections

This theme links all the sub-sections of the Department, for behind each collection, be it archaeology, ethnography, arms and armour or history, there is a collector, each one motivated in his own way to acquire objects, either in the course of their work or in what can only be inadequately described as a hobby.

Many of the early collectors of ethnographical objects can be associated with the spread of British colonial power in the last quarter of the 19th century, particularly in Africa. Amongst these were Joseph Moloney, medical officer to the expedition to S.E. Congo (Zaire) in 1891/2 and Sir Archibald Alison, associated with the British Punitive Expedition against the Ashanti in 1874. Missionaries, doctors, steamboat navigators all collected curios which they later presented to the Museum.

The famed ability of Scots to venture to remote parts of the world is illustrated by the intrepid Mrs Wilkie of Edinburgh who, after visiting her brother-in-law, a bishop, in Alaska in 1901, brought back an important collection of Eskimo and North West Coast Indian objects. Yet another was Robert Bruce, a former Glasgow yacht builder, who lived and worked with his brother in the Torres Straits between Australia and New Guinea towards the end of the 19th century. He gave the Museum in 1889 a large and important group of objects collected in New Guinea and the Torres Straits before the impact of white traders and missionaries had had much effect on those cultures.

In archaeology, also, early collectors were at work. Sir Robert Hamilton Lang, manager of the Ottoman Imperial Bank's Agency in Cyprus, and Her Majesty's Consul from 1871 to 1872, was collecting Cypriote antiquities as early as 1869 or 1870 and bequeathed part of his collection to Glasgow in 1903. Another was James Stevenson, a chemical manufacturer involved in the extraction of sulphur in the Lipari Islands, north of Sicily, who acquired pottery excavated in 1879 from the tombs of Greek colonists of the 4th century B.C. In contrast to Lang and Stevenson, with their limited interest in archaeology, was William Flinders Petrie who, while working for the Egypt Exploration Fund and later for the British School of Archaeology in Egypt, taught archaeologists that chronological evidence could be gained from examining the minutiae of excavations such as beads, potsherds and amulets. He was an innovator both in techniques of excavating and in the systematic analysis of objects from excavations and had a major impact on the development of archaeological thought towards the end of the 19th century. His achievements were honoured by a knighthood in 1923.

It is salutary to remember that a number of these early collections were made under unusual or hazardous conditions. Egypt in 1883, when the Egypt Exploration Fund began excavating there, was a country of considerable unrest and disorder. The Egyptian army had been in revolt and British troops had been sent in to quell the rebellion, culminating in the Battle of Tel-el-Kebir in September 1882. Thereafter, British troops occupied the country.

Hamilton Lang's problem was how to get the larger items from his collection out of Cyprus, which was under Turkish rule until it was ceded to the British in 1878. He had no *firman*, or imperial permission to export them, but, with a certain amount of ingenuity and cunning as well as the connivance of the local dragoman and the master of an English steamer, he managed to bring the bulk of his collection to Britain.

The last group of collectors to be considered belong to the last decades of the 19th and the early parts of the 20th century. They appear to have little in common, ranging from a rich man who collected European armour to another of more modest means who collected archaeological objects of Scottish origin. Each of the four was a polymath, however, with wide and varying cultural and sporting interests, apart from his professional career.

Robert Lyons Scott was a shipbuilder. He was also a great traveller, a renowned big game hunter (many of his trophies being in the McLean Museum in Greenock, his home town), a keen angler, yachtsman and fencer. He had an all-embracing knowledge of European armour and weapons and of related books, which he put to good use in his purchasing policy.

Charles Whitelaw was an architect, whose interest in, and knowledge of, Scottish weapons brought him into contact with Scott. His other interest in history and archaeology involved him in lecturing and writing for the Glasgow Archaeological Society and working for the preservation of Provand's Lordship, Glasgow's oldest house. He took part in excavations at Dunagoil in Bute, and this was his point of contact with the third collector of the group, Ludovic MacLellan Mann.

Mann was trained in accountancy and insurance, becoming chairman of a Glasgow and London firm of insurance brokers. He had a long-standing interest in archaeology and history, having been president of both the Glasgow Archaeological Society and Provand's Lordship Society and organizer of the Prehistoric Section of the Scottish Exhibition of Natural History, Art and Industry held in Glasgow in 1911. He carried out small-scale excavations around Glasgow and Ayrshire and was a great publicist for archaeology, both in radio talks and in articles for newspapers.

Lewis Clapperton was also a chartered accountant, again with many sporting, civic and cultural interests, the latter probably bringing him into contact with Mann and Whitelaw. His interest in furniture and pewter may well have developed in the context of the revival of craftsmanship associated with William Morris and the development of the Arts and Crafts Movement towards the end of the 19th century.

These four bequests — by Scott and Whitelaw in 1939, Clapperton in 1947 and Mann in 1955 — were, and are likely to remain, the last of the major public benefactions to the Department's collections. The era of building up a collection, slowly and painstakingly, with the intention of presenting it to a public institution such as a museum, has largely gone, mainly because such collections now have considerable value in the saleroom. This is sad, not only for museums which can no longer acquire entire collections, but also as, in the break-up of a collection, something of the character of the collector, expressed in his life-long interest or even passion, is lost.

Archaeology

Egypt

Although the then Kelvingrove Museum began acquiring objects in 1870, it was not until 1877 that the first Egyptian objects were donated. These were seven casts of statues in the Cairo Museum and were given by the Museum of Science and Art in Edinburgh, which later became, in 1904, the Royal Scottish Museum. Over the next fifteen years, sporadic donations were made, culminating in 1891 in the gift of some sixty objects, mostly funerary. These had been collected by John Galloway, a ship and insurance broker with the Glasgow firm of Patrick Henderson, and may have been donated on his retirement and removal to Ardrossan. In 1903, he presented a second group of objects which he had bought on a visit to Egypt. Galloway was a keen amateur Egyptologist who subscribed to the Glasgow Branch of the Egypt Exploration Fund. In letters which have been dated to 1892, he was encouraging Glasgow's councillors to send a Museum curator to Egypt to buy antiquities 'before prices go up and objects become rarer'.

Amongst the objects in Galloway's collection is a wooden coffin containing a mummified body [1] which dates from the late Dynastic or early Ptolemaic period of c.500 to 200 B.C. The body has a painted cartonnage mask, the use of which was widespread from the New Kingdom onwards, the cartonnage being made from strips of linen soaked in plaster which then hardened like a cast. The Museum register for 1891 records this object as 'mummy of a young man from Thebes'. Since then, however, the body has been X-rayed, and the radiographs indicate that it is more likely to be that of an elderly person and probably female.

In the 19th century, interest in Egyptology in Britain was fostered by the foundation in 1882 of the Egypt Exploration Fund which carried out annual excavations in Egypt. Its funds were raised by subscriptions from individuals, universities and institutions, and by 1894 there were 29 local branches throughout Britain, ranging from Dundee to Weston-super-Mare, as well as a very active American Branch. In proportion to the amount of subscription they paid, institutions such as museums received quotas of finds from each

1. *Detail of mummy with cartonnage mask, late Dynastic or early Ptolemaic c.500-200 B.C., length 157.5cm (62in).*

2. Predynastic painted pots, c.3500-3100 B.C., height of tallest 16.5cm (6½in).

season's excavation, thus enabling them to build up their collections of Egyptian antiquities. Glasgow first subscribed to the Fund in 1892, beginning a fruitful period of acquisition which lasted until the First World War.

Glasgow's collection reflects the historical sequence of excavations carried out by the Fund, starting with small groups of finds from sites such as Naukratis in the Nile Delta, an area of initial interest because of its association with Biblical places. The major period of acquisitions from the Fund was between 1898 and 1905, with finds from Dendereh, Diospolis Parva (modern Hu), Abydos, Deir el Bahri and Oxyrhynchus (modern Bahnasa). In 1899 the Fund allocated to Glasgow about 125 objects, mainly pottery from Hu. Almost one-third of these were predynastic pots, many with painted decoration [2], which were excavated by Flinders Petrie, who used the pottery from Hu and from a previous excavation at Naquada to work out a system he called 'sequence dating', which for the first time allowed finds to be classified by date and by type.

From 1899 the Fund began a long-standing and successful connection with Abydos, where sites ranged from royal tombs of the 1st Dynasty, c.3100 B.C., to remains dating from the Roman occupation of Egypt. Between 1900 and 1903 Glasgow acquired a considerable number of objects from Abydos, illustrated by a selection of finds from the tomb of a woman, Henut-taneb, of the 18th Dynasty [3]. The *shawabti* is typical of the kind of figures which were included in burials to act as servants to the dead person, by carrying out any tasks requiring to be done in the afterlife.

William Flinders Petrie (1853-1942) was the major archaeologist associated with the work of the Fund, and he directed excavations from 1883 to 1886 and again from 1896 to 1905. His programme of work would have daunted lesser people. Each season began for him in Egypt with excavation during the winter months, followed by the cataloguing and packing of finds before the return to Britain to write progress and excavation reports and to give lectures to promote the Fund's work.

From 1906 Petrie directed excavations on behalf of the British School of Archaeology in Egypt. During the 1912-13 season at Tarkhan, some 40 miles south of Cairo, he uncovered a series of burials of the early Dynastic period, which are particularly important for their

3. Shawabti figure, pot and beads from 18th Dynasty tomb of Henut-taneb, Abydos, c.1567-1320 B.C., height of figure 20cm (7⅞in).

4. Alabaster jar and small dish from Tarkhan, 1st Dynasty c.3100-2890 B.C., diameter of jar 13.8cm (5⅜in).

5. Painted wooden coffin of a priest, Nakht, from Beni Hasan, late 12th Dynasty c.1991- 1786 B.C., length 100cm (39¾in).

6. Amulets, beads and carved figures from el- Lahun, 23rd Dynasty 818-715 B.C., outside diameter of necklace 6.4cm (2½in).

7. Seated figure of a man, from el-Haraga, 11th-12th Dynasty c.2133-1786 B.C., height 28.5cm (11¼in).

preserved wooden beds, coffins and basketwork. The site also provided a wide range of pottery and stone vessels, which allowed Petrie to continue his work of classifying and dating, using his early Dynastic finds from Abydos as a guide [4].

Among the next season's excavations were those at el-Lahun and el-Haraga. From el-Lahun came grave goods of the 23rd Dynasty, showing the range of stones that were used in the making of amulets and jewellery. Rock crystal, carnelian and amethyst all feature, one stone being plated with gold [6]. El-Haraga produced 12th Dynasty material, including a finely sculptured seated figure of a dead man wrapped in a long cloak [7], whose detail and quality of workmanship is typical of the best of Middle Kingdom art.

The finds from el-Lahun and el-Haraga were given to the Museum by Flinders Petrie on behalf of the J. May Buchanan Collection. In the early part of the 20th century Miss J. May Buchanan was a most enthusiastic local Honorary Treasurer of the British School of Archaeology in Egypt, and during 1912 she organized a wide-ranging exhibition of Egyptian antiquities in the Art Gallery and Museum in Glasgow. Following her untimely death in December 1912, it was decided that donations of objects to the Egyptian collection would be made in memory of her work. As late as 1923, the Glasgow branch of the Egyptian Research Students Association donated to the collection finds from Abydos, Esneh, Kostameh and Beni Hasan. From this last site came a 12th Dynasty painted wooden coffin of a priest, Nakht [5]. The overall decoration is in accordance with Middle Kingdom coffins, incorporating two sacred eyes, invocations to Anubis and Osiris, and, painted on the lid, the skin of a leopard, emblem of the priesthood. The coffin is, however, only one metre long and contained only bones and a skull, so it is likely that the original burial of Nakht was disturbed, possibly by tomb robbers, and the remains later put in a box specially made for them.

Another donor to the Egyptian collections was the Reverend Colin Campbell who in 1913 presented a considerable number of inscribed stones from Abydos, Deir el Bahri and Dendereh, along with twelve funerary cones, supplemented in 1922 by another ten. These cones were part of the façade of private tombs. They were fixed to the walls by wedging the pointed end into the brickwork, leaving visible the flat end inscribed with the owner's name. Of particular interest is the fragment of a stele which commemorates Senenmut, chief steward to Queen Hatshepsut (1490-1468 B.C.) [8] and in charge of the estates of the ruler and of the royal family, a position of great responsibility. Senenmut is shown making an offering of a burnt goose or duck, presumably to a god.

The largest, and certainly the heaviest, donation came in 1922 when the Hamilton Estates Trustees presented to the Museum the granite sarcophagus [9], or coffin, of Pa-Ba-Sa, a high official of King Psamtek I who reigned from 664 to 609 B.C. He was master of the whole priesthood of Egypt, controlling the wealth of the temples. This sarcophagus is one of two acquired by the 10th Duke of Hamilton (1767-1852) and probably stood in the Egyptian Hall of Hamilton Palace, although its history there has yet to be unravelled. The other sarcophagus was used for the Duke's interment in the mausoleum of the Palace in 1852. When the mausoleum went out of use in the 1920s, the Duke, still interred in his Egyptian coffin, was buried nearby, in Hamilton.

8. *Stele of Senenmut from Karnak, 18th Dynasty c.1489-1480 B.C., height 21cm (8¼in).*

9. *Detail of granite sarcophagus of Pa-Ba-Sa, 26th Dynasty c.664-525 B.C., length 214cm (84¼in).*

Cyprus

Some three hundred Cypriote objects, initially given on loan in 1870, were donated to the Museum in 1903 by Sir Robert Hamilton Lang. This important group consists of about 170 pieces of pottery, mainly of the Bronze Age, a small number of bronze weapons, and over one hundred glass vessels of the Graeco-Roman period.

Hamilton Lang was manager of the Imperial Ottoman Bank's Agency in Cyprus from 1863 to 1872, combining this with the post of Her Majesty's Consul from 1871 to 1872. Initially he had little interest in archaeology but from 1868 onwards he was carrying out excavations.

Included in the Lang collection is a ceramic model throne [1], the painted lattice decoration probably imitating the thongs of a seat. Models of thrones are rare in Cyprus, and this example is unusual because of its large size.

Another ceramic piece, the stirrup jar decorated with geometric motifs [2], is the commonest form of white-painted pottery ware and is found throughout Cyprus during the Middle Bronze Age. The jug [2] belongs to the Archaic Period (*c*.750-650 B.C.). The stylized bird in its decoration is typical of the 'free-field' style and is derived from Syrian and Phoenician sources.

Unfortunately, as yet little is known of the provenance of the Graeco-Roman glass pieces, two of which are shown here [2], but they may have been found in the cemeteries at Laksha Nicoli.

1. *Ceramic model throne, Early Geometric period* c. *900-800* B.C., *height 18.6cm (7⅜in).*

2. *Decorated jug, Archaic Period* c. *750-650* B.C.; *stirrup jar, middle Bronze Age* c. *1900-1625* B.C.; *two glass vessels,* c. *500-100* B.C.; *height of stirrup jar 17.8cm (7in).*

Italian-Greek Colonies

The Museum has an important collection of pottery from Lipari, the largest of seven islands off the north coast of Sicily, an area colonized by the Greeks early in the 6th century B.C.

James Stevenson of Hailie, Largs, a partner in the firm of Stevenson, Carlile & Co, chemical manufacturers, is thought to have been the owner of a sulphur mine on Vulcano, an island close to Lipari. In 1879 he acquired the contents of tombs excavated there and in 1885 deposited them on loan to the Museum. On his death in 1903 they were bequeathed to the Museum.

1. Ceramic calyx-crater, height 91cm (35¾in).

2. Marriage vase, lidded cup and shallow lidded dish, 4th century B.C., height of vase 46cm (18¼in).

An important pottery workshop was operating on Lipari between *c.*350 and 300 B.C. A number of the vessels can be attributed to a particular artist, known to modern archaeologists as the 'Lipari Painter', who was working at the end of the 4th century B.C. The marriage vase, the lidded cup and the shallow lidded dish [2] illustrate elements of his style in the use of an individual palmette and the figures, which include, on the vase, a seated woman, one arm resting on a pillar or the arm of a chair, and, on the cup, female heads in profile.

The calyx-crater [1], used for mixing wine with water, is a rare object. The bearded, male head is named AKRATOS, said to be one of the attendants of Dionysius. The vessel may have been an import from Cumae on the Italian mainland.

1. *Gavel Moss hoard of bronze dagger and axeheads, early Bronze Age c.1600-1500 B.C., length of dagger 25.7cm (10⅛in).*

Scotland

Archaeological collections reflect more often the various methods of acquiring objects rather than the interests of major collectors, although the name of Ludovic MacLellan Mann does stand out as one of the department's major benefactors.

The first archaeological object acquired by the Museum in 1872 was, appropriately, a stone axe, 'found in 1848 at corner of Sauchiehall and Buchanan Streets' in Glasgow. The first purchase by the department was made in 1890 and consisted of two stone balls from Aberdeenshire and three flints from Ireland. For a short period up to the turn of the century, purchases increased. The year 1892 saw the purchase of objects from Orkney and, in a saleroom in Edinburgh in November 1892, the museum bought part of the collection of John Rae of Aberdeen, much of which was of north-east origin. From 1894 to 1896 flint and stone tools and pottery from Sweden, Denmark, Switzerland, France and Ireland were bought. After 1900 the emphasis returned to donations. In 1902 some 130 items were presented by the Governors of the then Glasgow and West of Scotland Technical College, the Andersonian Collection.

Objects of archaeological interest are occasionally found by accident, as the result of digging a garden or spotted on a hillwalk. These are referred to as casual or isolated finds, that is, they have no association with other objects or structural remains. Farming activities frequently uncover such finds. In 1790 a dagger and two axeheads were ploughed up on Gavel Moss Farm, near Lochwinnoch in Renfrewshire [1]. A family tradition suggests that 'armour' was found also but if so this was not preserved. The farmer who found the objects gave them to his niece as a wedding present in 1810, and her great-grandson first loaned them and eventually sold them to the Museum in 1959. The ribbed dagger and the axes, one decorated with a chevron motif, date from the early Bronze Age, c.1600-1500 B.C. These pieces may have been the personal belongings of one man.

More recently, in the 1960s, farming activity at Badden Farm, north of Lochgilphead in Argyll, brought to light a large stone slab decorated with multiple lozenge patterns [2]. The slab would have formed one side of a rectangular stone coffin, or cist, for a body of the early or middle Bronze Age. Apart from the decoration, unusual features are the two vertical grooves and the rebating on the bottom, indicating woodworking techniques translated into stonework.

2. *Badden cist slab, early Bronze Age c.1800-1500 B.C., length 151.5cm (59⅝in).*

Even now, archaeological objects tend to have no monetary value, but occasionally items have to be bought to fill an important gap in a collection. A Neolithic jadeite axe from near Glenluce in Galloway was purchased, and another, from the Dumbrock Estate, Strathblane, was an exchange with another museum [4]. Stone axes of the Neolithic period were functional objects used to cut down small trees, to clear undergrowth or dress wood. Jadeite, a greenish stone brought into Britain from western Europe, was used for axes where colour and a high quality of finish were more important than utilitarian function. Such axes must have had a symbolic role, although whether to indicate power, for use in religious ritual, or for exchange between Neolithic communities, is uncertain.

Excavation, in Scotland as elsewhere, has always been a major source of objects for museums. Until the 1930s and 1940s many excavations were carried out by amateur archaeologists, that is, people with their own professions, who had a keen and active interest in archaeology. In this way two food vessels and a cinerary urn [3] were excavated at Tomontend, on the island of Great Cumbrae, in 1878. The site was a large stone cairn, sixty feet in diameter. Near the centre of the cairn, the excavators found one food vessel in a stone cist with the remains of a cremated burial. The other food vessel and the cinerary urn are the remnants of 'five large urns' found on the edge of the cairn. These were secondary burials inserted into the body of the cairn some time after the initial burial in the mid Bronze Age.

In 1921, gold ornaments dating from the late Bronze Age, c.700-600 B.C., were discovered at Whitefarland on Arran [5]. The solid gold cloak fastener was a casual find, and the small hair ornament of sheet gold and wire was unearthed in a follow-up investigation by two amateur archaeologists and the then Superintendent of Glasgow Museums. The cloak fastener had been sent by the finders to a Glasgow jeweller who, fortunately, showed it to someone with archaeological knowledge. Other instances have been recorded of gold ornaments being melted down for their gold content by jewellers ignorant of their historical importance.

3. Food vessels and cinerary urn from Great Cumbrae, early or middle Bronze Age c.1800-1200 B.C., height of urn 20cm (7⅞in).

4. Jadeite axeheads from Dumbrock Estate, Strathblane, and Glengorrie Farm, Glenluce, late Neolithic c.2800-2000 B.C., length of Glengorrie Farm axehead 15.1cm (5⅞in).

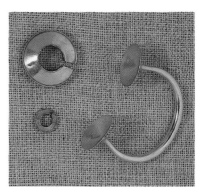

5. Gold cloak fastener and hair ornament from Arran, hair ornament from Glenluce, late Bronze Age c.700-600 B.C., diameter of cloak fastener 7.7cm (3in).

6. *Reconstructed jet necklace from Brackley, Kintyre, early Bronze Age c.1700-1400 B.C., diameter 28cm (11in).*

7. *Carved stone balls from Aboyne, Alford and Inverurie, Aberdeenshire, late Neolithic c.2500-2000 B.C., diameter of largest 7.8cm (3in).*

The advent of full-time professional archaeologists working for government agencies, local authorities, universities and other public bodies has led to an increase in the scientific investigation of archaeological sites. Museums have benefited from this by acquiring an excavation's finds, either through donation by the landowner or, in recent years, through a Finds Disposal Panel which allocates finds from excavations funded by the Scottish Development Department (Historic Buildings and Monuments).

In 1952 and 1953 Mr Jack Scott, then the Museum archaeologist, excavated a Neolithic chambered cairn at Brackley in Kintyre. In the primary burial chamber he uncovered a secondary burial dating from the early Bronze Age, c.1700-1400 B.C., which had been inserted into the Neolithic chamber. The finds from the secondary burial included fragments of a food vessel, a flint knife, flint and pitchstone tools and an incomplete jet necklace, now reconstructed [6]. The pieces of jet were worn, some even damaged, and two of the flat spacer plates were from a different necklace. Obviously, jet necklaces in the Bronze Age were highly prized or were of such significance that worn-out pieces were buried with the dead.

The largest collection of Scottish objects was bequeathed by Ludovic MacLellan Mann (1869-1955), an amateur archaeologist who by training and profession was an accountant and insurance broker. His archaeological and historical interests were wide and varied. He organized the Prehistoric Section of the 1911 Historical Exhibition in Glasgow and in the late 1920s was also involved with setting up the Museum's collections. He maintained contacts with others of a like mind throughout the west of Scotland, particularly in Dumfries and Galloway, who kept him informed of archaeological finds. As a result he built up wide-ranging collections of objects from prehistoric to post-Roman and early Medieval times. Part of his collection are mysterious carved stone balls of the late Neolithic period which appear to have no utilitarian function [7]. They have been found in large numbers, particularly in the north-east of Scotland, but have little or no association with other objects or structures.

Ethnography

Glasgow's ethnography collection has been built up in four ways. Donations by individual collectors, ranging from one or two objects to several hundred, have always been important, while many excellent additions have been made by direct purchase. The Museum has also benefited from gifts from other institutions, and from time to time important items have been loaned. In the present display the nearly eight hundred objects derive from more than two hundred separate sources, yet represent only a fraction of the Museum's total holding. The earliest acquisitions were made in the 1870s, the founding decade of the Museum, and include a gift of African material bearing the neatly written tag, 'Collected by Dr Livingstone and bequeathed by T.S. Livingstone'.

1. *BaLuba caryatid stools (Moloney's stool on left), Zaire, height 47.3cm (18⅝in).*

Africa

The African collection is wide-ranging and includes the implements and ornaments of everyday life and also ritual and ceremonial carvings. The cultures covered include the Bushmen hunter-gatherers of the south; the pastoral nomads of the east, such as the Masai; the agricultural Bantu-speaking peoples of the Congo in Central Africa; and the complex civilizations of West Africa with the main strength of the collection in the latter two areas.

The origins of the Congo group of objects illustrate the degree to which ethnography is a child of 19th-century colonialism, for of the two early collections which figure strongly in the present Central Africa display, one was made by a member of a military expedition and the other by a member of a missionary organization.

Joseph Moloney was medical officer on an expedition in 1891 to Katanga, in the southeast of the Congo (now Zaire), to set up mines and to obtain Belgian sovereignty over that part of the Congo. Moloney wrote a book about the hazards of the journey which showed scant interest in the societies through which he passed and did not even mention the 27 objects he brought back with him and donated to the Museum in 1907. Throughout Africa, stools have political and religious significance and in different cultures are carved in distinctive ways. The caryatid stool collected by Moloney [1], with its rounded form, elongated arms, tribal marks and serene expression was carved from a single block of wood. It is especially typical of the BaLuba people of southeastern Zaire and indicated the rank of chief. It may well be one of the earliest collected in the BaLuba region.

2. *BaKuba mask, Zaire?, height 38cm (15in).*

'I have been in Central Africa on the Congo and Kessai rivers in charge of a mission steamer for some time, and during that time I have collected a good number of curiosities from different points.' Thus began W.B. Scott's letter to the Museum in September 1910; later in that year he sold about 170 objects. These included weapons, various implements and ornaments, some vessels shaped in human form, and a beaded BaKuba mask [2] from the area which is now central Zaire. The BaKuba was a prosperous federation of tribes which recognized a divine king and claimed a very ancient ancestry. The venerated Shamba (1600-20), who began a tradition of carving

3. *BaLuba kifwebe mask, Zaire, depth to chin 43.2cm (17in).*

figures of successive rulers, was held to be the 93rd king. Carvers and blacksmiths achieved the highest grades of the aristocracy in this area, and cloth-making was a royal monopoly. The art and artefacts of the BaKuba were thus strongly focussed on the king and his court.

In BaKuba oral history, Bo Kena, the 73rd king, is said to have invented a mask of the 'Mashamboy' type, with a flat face of antelope skin, a wooden nose, and eyes and face of beads and cowrie shells. It may have been worn in commemoration of a distant ancestor or used in the initiation rituals undergone by youths.

On display with it is a BaLuba mask of the *kifwebe* type [3], so named after a secret society. Interpretations of this mask too differ, but it probably also figured in initiation ceremonies. The uncertainty about the meaning of masks reflects both differences in the use of similar masks between neighbouring peoples and the lack of good documentation of objects by early collectors. The geometric grooved patterns and spherical shape make these BaLuba masks distinctive, and they are found with and without the raffia beard.

The courtly art of West Africa aroused great interest on its arrival in Europe in the early 20th century. A punitive British military expedition, taking reprisal for the killing of a party led by the British Vice-Consul, raided Benin City in 1897 and sent back more than two thousand bronze castings, ivory carvings and other pieces. The power and serenity of many of the figures and heads led some at the time misguidedly to seek Greek origins. It is now recognized that the art of such kingdoms as Ife and Benin in Nigeria and the Ashanti in neighbouring Ghana was wholly that of black Africa, and the cultures date back at least to the beginning of the Christian era in the West.

In the 18th century, the Ashanti reached the height of their power over large areas of what is now Ghana and the Ivory Coast. The basis of their expansion lay in rich gold mines which enabled them to trade gold north across the Sahara and south to early European voyagers. Early visitors have left vivid accounts of the splendour and order of the capital Kumasi, and of the profusion of gold items there [4].

4. *Ashanti miniature figures with brass weights for weighing gold, Ghana, height of tallest figure 7cm (2¾in).*

5. *Two Benin bronze portrait heads, height of 'winged' head 51.5cm (20¼in).*

Two Benin bronze heads were bought at auction in Glasgow in 1901, four years after the Punitive Raid [5]. Such *loba* heads of a deceased ruler were traditionally commissioned by his successor and placed on an altar as the focus for commemorative rituals. They have been expertly cast by the court brass-smiths to show coral and agate beads, tribal scars and, on the flanged base, animal motifs. The larger head, with the 'winged' cap, is among the largest Benin heads known anywhere, and probably dates from the mid-19th century. The smaller one is probably from the second half of the 18th century.

On the swampy eastern side of the Niger delta, in Nigeria, live the Kalabari Ijaw. They are mainly fishermen but also carry out some cultivation, living in a state of some size. Formerly they were feared among neighbouring peoples as slave-raiders. Anthropologists have been particularly interested in the sophisticated and complex cosmological beliefs held by the Kalabari Ijaw. This system includes three orders of existence beyond 'the place of people', one of which is a spirit world inhabited by a variety of spiritual beings, with whom contact is made through ritual. The funerary screen, or *duen fobara* [6], is a memorial to a dead chief or ancestor, set up by his successor. This example is interesting in two ways. First, it is assembled from numerous separate pieces of carved wood, and not carved from a single block, as is more usual in African art. Secondly, its construction shows how, within a traditional context, African craftsmen adopted designs and techniques from other cultures. The carpentry technique probably stems from contact with European ships, while the arrangement of the figures seems similar to a Benin bronze plaque, perhaps seen by the Ijaw only in woodcut prints in European books. This screen, given by James Newall Thompson in 1900, is particularly elaborate and probably dates from the second half of the 19th century. It depicts a chief and two attendants. The row of heads probably represents the chief's slaves. Two are possibly wearing *otobo* masks, which represent a hippopotamus-like water spirit and are examples of a mask which faced upwards and was not intended to be seen.

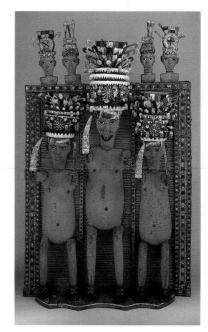

6. *Kalabari Ijaw funerary screen, Nigeria, height 156.2cm (61¼in).*

Oceania

Of the main island groups of the Pacific, the Torres Straits islands, between New Guinea and the northern tip of Australia, are of special interest to anthropologists, since it was here, in 1898, that the first specifically anthropological field-work expedition was undertaken by A.C. Haddon. He had, however, been preceded in the islands by a number of missionaries and teachers, among whom was Robert Bruce, a former Glasgow yacht-builder, who lived and taught with his brother on the islands and gave 150 objects to the Museum in 1889, forming one of the most outstanding Torres Straits collections in the world. As with many parts of Oceania, relatively small areas in the Torres Straits produced an astonishing range and quantity of arts and artefacts. Masks, representing spirits, were a vital part of the ritual life which centered on the 'men's house', and were said to induce awe and terror in the uninitiated. The mask here is made of wood, cassowary feathers and vegetable fibre [7]. It may have been associated with initiation rituals, or with a ritual that followed the harvest of wild plums in the autumn.

Music, singing and dancing were associated with both ritual and

7. *Mask and drum, Torres Straits, height of mask 94cm (37in).*

8. *Maori figure of a man, New Zealand, height 47cm (18¾in).*

9. *Ceremonial Eskimo suit of caribou skin and wolverine fur, Alaska, height 166.4cm (65½in).*

entertainment. Drums of roughly similar shape are found throughout Melanesia, but the Torres Straits *warup* drum is distinctive [7]. Made of wood, with cassowary feathers and a membrane of lizard skin for beating with the hands, the pitch could be altered by adding lumps of wax to the skin. The mouth is carved to resemble a fish.

New Zealand forms the southern angle of the giant triangle of the islands of Polynesia. The Maori tribes trace their ancestry back to the legendary voyagers who settled in New Zealand from islands to the north. Traditionally their society was divided into slaves, commoners and nobles. As in all Polynesia, social life was permeated with the two strong mystical forces of 'mana' and 'tapu' (the origin of the word taboo). The Maori figure shown here [8] is extremely unusual as it is more naturalistic than much Maori carving. Only a few of such free-standing figures are known anywhere in the world (another is also in Glasgow, in the Hunterian Museum). The figure is male, has human hair, claw-like hands, *moko* tattoo and concave adze-marks on the wood surface. It was given in 1948 by Mr S.N. Folker, and the family history of the figure has an appropriate semi-legendary air. It was stolen by Samuel Folker, of Felstead in Essex, a midshipman serving under Nelson in about 1780. The details of geography are doubtful in the story, but the date seems very likely, making the figure one of the oldest surviving Maori carvings. Experts have disagreed as to its original function. It may well be a symbol of one of the many Maori gods or equally it may be a house-post image from the time when images were bound to a pole, and not, as later, carved directly out of the wood of the house. If this is the case, it is probably of a non-deified ancestor.

The Americas

The Eskimo, or Inuit and Aleut peoples, now number fewer than 100,000, but, as a more or less unified cultural group, they still stretch over an enormous area, from Greenland across Arctic Russia into North America. With peoples like the Bushmen of southern Africa, they represent supreme examples of the human capacity to adapt to the harshest environments, making maximum use of the materials available around them: animal skin and bone, stone and snow.

In an environment where the temperature is below freezing point for most of the year, clothing is obviously of great importance, and the suit, expertly made by Eskimo women, conserves body heat with an efficiency hardly matched by Western methods and materials. This example [9] is made of caribou skin with a hood edged with wolverine fur, which does not freeze up. The skin is sewn together with leather thongs and whale sinew thread. It is of finer quality than everyday wear and would probably have been worn for ceremonies or for visiting. Other interesting Eskimo garments can be seen in the permanent display, including a waterproof suit made from seal intestines. The suit is part of an excellent collection sold by Mrs E.M. Wilkie, of Edinburgh. In May 1901 she wrote to the Museum, 'May I draw your attention to a collection which I made in Alaska last year when I was visiting my brother-in-law, Bishop Rowe?' Her letter reveals that some of her 55 objects were bought from Lieutenant G.T. Emmons, who did much to conserve Eskimo and Indian cultures and ensured that many of their artefacts are now in museums.

Mrs Wilkie's collection also included objects from other North American Indian cultures. At Kelvingrove, four major groups are well represented: the Eastern Woodland Indians, such as the Iroquois, who were cultivators with a highly organized system of government; the buffalo-hunters and warriors of the Plains, such as the Sioux; the Pueblo or village-dwelling Indians of the Southwest; and the Indians of the North West Coast of Canada.

The culture of the North West Coast Indians was unusual, for their hunting-gathering economy was rich enough to allow both an elaborate system of social ranks and the time to organize large-scale rituals and tremendous feasts. A principal tribe of the area, the Kwakiutl, was particularly known for an extraordinary feast called the 'potlatch'. Chiefs vied with each other not in accumulating wealth, but by giving it away ostentatiously at such feasts, and indeed by consigning boxes, blankets and even canoes to giant bonfires.

The motifs of North West Coast Indian art are instantly recognizable: curvilinear, two-dimensional, symmetrical designs, often of animals, stylized and inter-locking. Common animals are the bear, the raven, the whale, the eagle and the beaver, and they are depicted on cedar-wood chests, blankets, the handles of goat-horn spoons, house-posts and totem-poles, wooden masks and basketry hats [10]. Produced for dramatic ceremonies, and functioning as symbols of status and as representations of the supernatural world, these objects reveal superb aesthetic quality, as can be seen in the Haida skin apron [12] and the Tlingit 'Chilkat' blanket [11].

The apron was worn in dances, either of a religious or a secular kind. The puffin beaks and deer hooves hanging from the fringe would have made an exciting jingling sound as the dancer moved. This apron was given by the Museum of the Wellcome Institute for the History of Medicine, from whom Kelvingrove obtained a large number of excellent ethnographic objects in the 1950s. It probably dates from the late 19th century. The Chilkat blanket or cloak would have been worn at important ceremonies by both sexes. It might have taken a year to make, woven by women on a 'half-loom', the warp material being a core of shredded cedar bark wrapped in mountain goat wool.

10. *North West Coast basketry hat, Alaska, height 33cm (13in).*

11. *Detail of Chilkat blanket, Alaska, width 132cm (52in).*

12. *Haida skin apron, Alaska, depth 63.5cm (25in).*

13. *Bronze figure of Lakshmi, India, 14th century; soapstone carving of an Immortal, China, Ming Dynasty 1368-1644; figure of the Buddha, Burma, 16th or 17th century; bronze figure of Krishna, Indian, early 16th century; height of Buddha 22cm (8¾in).*

Asia

When considering Asia, anthropologists sometimes distinguish between the cultures of the Great Tradition, characterized by state-systems and the presence of an ethical, literate, 'world religion', such as Hinduism or Buddhism (or Christianity), and the Little Tradition, where a non-literate religious system is associated with the local gods and spirits.

The divine in Hinduism is represented in a trinity of gods: Brahma, the creative element; Vishnu, the conserving; and Shiva, the destroying. Vishnu protects the world, both from on high and by descending to earth in human or animal incarnations, *avatars*. Krishna is one human avatar of Vishnu: a powerful god, but sometimes mischievous and altogether rather human. In this early 16th-century bronze figure [13], Krishna is seen as a youth playing the flute with which he charmed women. He is shown with a calf, recalling the myth that he grew up among cowherds to avoid the anger of his uncle. Vishnu's consort was the independent-minded Lakshmi, the goddess of fortune and prosperity, who accompanied him in most of his incarnations. In this 14th-century bronze figure [13], Lakshmi stands on a lotus pedestal in the graceful triple flexion stance, holding her symbol, the lotus, in her right hand and with her left hand posed like an elephant's trunk. These two objects were given in 1929 by Mr James Boyd of Lenzie, and are part of a very considerable gift of more than a hundred buddhas and deities, collected on various trips.

Philosophy and religion form the theme of much Chinese art. Several thinkers founded traditions in the turbulent period of the Warring States (475-221 B.C.), including Confucius and Lao-Tze, the founder of Taoism. These and later influences, such as Buddhism, co-existed with ancestor-worship. Confucianism is less a religion than a system of ethics and philosophy, closely tied to the needs of the Chinese bureaucracy. Taoism also began as a philosophy, but acquired magical and mythological elements, among which were the Immortals, depicted in painting and popularized in sculpture since the Ming period of the 14th to 17th centuries. The Immortal depicted in this 18th or 19th-century soapstone carving [13] is seen reclining in a woody grove.

Buddhism originated in India with the teachings of the Buddha Sakyamuni (560-480 B.C.), but it has spread to cover a wide part of Asia, including Burma, from where this 16th or 17th-century seated Buddha comes [13]. The depiction of the Buddha in art follows a number of stylistic rules concerning posture and dress. In this figure, the Buddha is seated in the *bhumisparsamudra* pose which recalls the story of his defeat of the demon Mara.

The model of a warrior from Japan [14] shows a costume typical of the Momoyama Period, the second half of the 16th century and the beginning of the 17th, when there was weak central government and *daimyo* barons and their *samurai* warriors battled for power. This samurai wears a long sword or *tachi* and carries a polearm or *hoko*, which he would have swung standing up in the saddle. The emblem in his right hand signifies the rank of a general. The samurai's armour was made from strips of lacquered metal with leather and silk lacing, clearly reproduced on this model which was bought from Mr Thomas B. Lindsay, a former member of the Education staff at the Museum.

14. *Model of a samurai warrior, Japan, height of figure 86.4cm (34in).*

History

The history collection is a glorious hotchpotch which includes coins and medals, snuff boxes, clocks, pewter, tartan, household and kitchen utensils, candlesticks and cruses, spinning wheels, agricultural implements and the robes of a Moderator of the General Assembly of the Church of Scotland. A few items have been chosen to highlight the range of the collection.

Snuff boxes

There are about five hundred snuff boxes in the history collections, including several important gifts. Sixty-four 'Jacobite' boxes, of a baluster-shaped construction peculiar to Scotland, were bequeathed in 1926 by ex-bailie Edward J. Thomson. One of these [1] is said to have belonged to James Francis Edward Stuart, the Old Pretender. On its silver and tortoiseshell staves are inlaid in gold, silver and mother-of-pearl, the Jacobite crowned thistle and crowned rose and a female figure identified as Clementina Sobieska, wife of the Old Pretender and mother of Bonnie Prince Charlie. Missing from this particular box is a male figure found on other boxes and presumed to be James. On the lid is a charming musical scene. Another similar box [1] has the Jacobite acorn and clasped hand symbols incised on two of its silver staves.

In 1950 a collection of over 360 snuff boxes and related material was given to the Museum by descendants of Alexander Moncrieff Mitchell, a prominent Glasgow lawyer. The collection includes European and Oriental material, but has a strong Scottish representation including examples of the typical horn mull. One simple cowhorn mull [2] has the tip crudely carved into the shape of a horse's head. Another, more sophisticated, commercially produced type, has silver mounts and a thistle-shaped hinge.

1. Silver and tortoiseshell baluster snuff box inlaid in gold, silver and mother-of-pearl; silver and tortoiseshell baluster box; Scottish?, 18th century, height of inlaid box 6cm (2¼in).

2. Cowhorn mull, 18th century; horn and silver mull, 19th century, both Scottish; height of cowhorn mull 9.5cm (3¾in).

3. *Orrery clock by Raingo, French, c.1820, height 76.2cm (30in).*

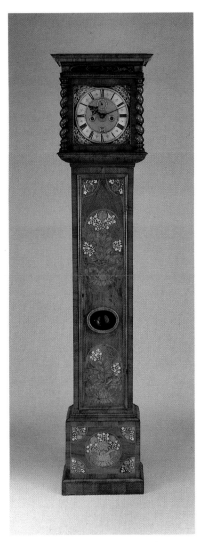

5. *Walnut veneered longcase clock with marquetry inlay, English, c.1690, height 194.3cm (76¼in).*

4. *Detail of orrery mechanism.*

Clocks

In the 1940s and 50s, Mr and Mrs William Brownhill Smith gave to the Museum a small but very fine collection of clocks, including an attractive 17th-century longcase clock [5]. In the second half of that century three developments had taken place in clockmaking; the introduction of the long pendulum, the anchor escapement and the long case which, when put together, produced the longcase clock. This clock, like all early examples, is small and narrow. The hood, which has no door, slides upwards for winding. The case is oak veneered in walnut and has inlaid marquetry panels in ivory and contrasting woods. The pendulum can be seen through a bull's-eye glass in the front of the case.

In 1900 a number of ethnographic items, mainly material collected in Central Africa by David Livingstone, were gifted to the Museum by the son of the collector, James Young. An exotic bedfellow accompanied these items: one of about a dozen orrery clocks made by Raingo of Paris around the 1820s [3]. Such clocks represent the highest point of the clockmaker's art and were often intended to be showpieces. One set of hands on the vertical face of the clock tells the time, while another indicates the day of the week and the symbol for the planet from which the day of the week is derived. The orrery on top [4] demonstrates the motions of the earth and moon in rotation around the sun. Such orrery mechanisms for showing planetary movements are named after the 4th Earl of Orrery, for whom the first one was made.

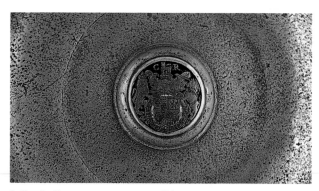

7. *Detail of boss on pewter rosewater dish.*

6. *Pewter rosewater dish with brass and enamel boss, English, early 17th century, diameter 45.7cm (18in).*

8. *Pewter communion flagons and christening basin, Scottish, 1795, height of flagons 27.3cm (10¾in).*

Pewter

Glasgow has one of the finest pewter collections in Britain, due largely to the generosity of a few important benefactors. Lewis Clapperton's bequest of 1947 is the most impressive. A local chartered accountant, Clapperton (1865-1947) typified the busy all-rounder of his day. He was a burgess of the City of Glasgow, a member of the Merchant's House, a Special Constable and a sergeant in the Glasgow Volunteer Regiment. His cultural interests included The Old Glasgow Club, Provand's Lordship Society and the National Trust for Scotland. He was a keen sportsman and served on many charitable committees.

Clapperton's collection is primarily a British one, but with a strong Scottish representation. His catalogue and correspondence are invaluable sources of information on the acquisition of each piece. The collection begins tentatively in the 1890s and includes the purchase in Reykjavik, Iceland, for five shillings of an unusual pocket communion set. Although Clapperton continued collecting until the outbreak of the Second World War, the bulk of his collection, about two-thirds of the whole, was acquired between 1900 and the outbreak of the First World War. At that time there was a general revival in interest in pewter collecting in Britain, and major exhibitions were organized at Clifford's Inn Hall, London, in 1904 and 1908. In 1909 Clapperton and others organized a Loan Exhibition of Old Pewter at Provand's Lordship in Glasgow, the oldest house in the city.

One of the most attractive items in the Clapperton collection is a

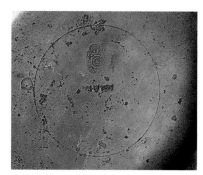

9. *Detail of mark on christening basin.*

10. *Pewter candlestick, English?, early 17th century, height 19cm (7¼in).*

11. *Pewter quaich, Scottish, late 17th century, diameter 12.7cm (5in).*

12. *St Kilda spinning wheel, 19th century, height 91.4cm (36in); blanket woven on St Kilda, 20th century, length 172.7cm (68in).*

large rosewater dish [6] with a central brass and enamel boss bearing the Royal Arms and cipher CR [7]. Before the widespread introduction of forks, such dishes were probably used for washing one's hands in scented water during the course of a meal. There are less than twenty known examples of these dishes, and this one came from Watermouth Castle in Devon.

In 1930, a small pewter candlestick was excavated in Scarborough, Yorkshire, and acquired by Clapperton. The candlestick, a rare 17th-century bell-based stick, is unmarked but probably English [10]. H.H. Cotterell, pewter dealer and writer, wrote: 'I rejoice with you over your triumph. There is no other word for it, for it appeals to me as one of the finest pieces I have ever handled, and that must be more than any man living or dead.'

Pewterware survived in use in Scotland, particularly as church plate, much later than it did in England. There are many Scottish communion cups and flagons to be found, but christening basins are much less common. Clapperton, however, acquired one from Muckhart Parish Church in Perthshire. It is inscribed MUCKART 1795 and is 'hallmarked' by James Wright of Edinburgh. In 1978 the church sent for sale at Sotheby's in London a pair of flagons similarly inscribed, and these were purchased for the collection [8]. The flagons are typical of Presbyterian church plate of the late 18th century, and also bear the 'hallmarks' of James Wright. However, the large maker's mark on the bowl, a crowned rose with EDINBURGH beneath [9], is not repeated on the flagons. They have an eagle on orb mark with the motto LIVE BY HOPE above. The two different makers' marks may have been used by Wright, but one may be that of an associate finishing or selling the product.

Quaichs, which are peculiarly Scottish drinking vessels, differ from the common English porringer in the curved shape of their interiors and in their solid lugs which are never pierced. They are familiar in wood and silver, but extremely rare in pewter. There is one unmarked late 17th-century example in the Clapperton Collection [11], which was purchased in 1923 for £30.

Folk Life

Because of Glasgow's strong links with the Western Highlands and Islands, a substantial collection of material relating to life in these areas has accumulated in the Museum. In the last few decades of the 19th century in particular, summer visitors on steamer excursions would bring back souvenirs of their visits. Traders, doctors, government officials and naval personnel, whose work took them north, also added to the collections.

Material from St Kilda, until its evacuation in 1930 the remotest inhabited island in the British Isles, includes snares for catching seabirds — the St Kildan staple diet — household equipment, clothing and the oldest spinning wheel on the island at the time of the evacuation [12]. It is a typical Scottish horizontal wheel and would have been imported to St Kilda, not made on the island. It was donated by Wilhelmina Barclay, Queen's Nurse on St Kilda from 1927 to 1930, who played a major role in organizing the evacuation of the last 36 St Kildans to the mainland.

Musical Instruments

The bulk of Glasgow's collection of musical instruments is formed by two collections, which were purchased in 1942 and 1945.

The Glen collection is part of one assembled by an Edinburgh instrument-making family. Begun by Thomas McBain Glen (1804-1873), it was one of the first collections of musical instruments to be made, and items from it appeared in most major exhibitions of instruments from 1872 on, including one in Glasgow in 1941.

A rare instrument is the transverse flute [13] of brown boxwood and ivory. Made in Paris, about 1710, by Jean Jacques Rippert, it is an example of the 'baroque' flute developed by Jean Hotteterre and others in Paris at the end of the 17th century. One of its most distinctive features is its construction in three sections, whereas previous flutes were made from one piece of wood.

The second collection was gathered by Dr Henry George Farmer (1882-1965). He started music lessons when he was seven and in 1896 joined the Royal Artillery band, later becoming musical director of the Broadway Theatre in London and then of the Coliseum and Empire Theatres in Glasgow. He was a noted musicologist, and as he had said he wished 'to see these instruments in Glasgow', some fifty instruments were offered and bought by the Museum.

Of these one of the most interesting is the dancing master's kit [14]. This instrument, which is a type of small fiddle, was made or sold by 'James Aird at his shop, [at] the corner of Gibson's Wynd [and] New Street' in Glasgow about 1780 and was eventually acquired by John Hall of Ayr (1788-1862). The kit (the word possibly comes from 'kitten') was used to teach dancing. It was small enough to be played while demonstrating dance steps and quiet enough not to disturb neighbours. It could also be placed in the pocket when not in use, hence its other name, the 'pochette'. At that time, dancing masters not only taught but also published music, and Hall, who was one of Glasgow's earliest music sellers, was responsible for two volumes. A manuscript book of his 'Quadrilles and Waltzes' [14] contains dances which may have been played on the kit.

13. Boxwood and ivory flute by Rippert, French, c.1710, length 65cm (25¼in).

14. Dancing master's kit fiddle, Scottish, c.1780; manuscript book of quadrilles and waltzes, Scottish, early 19th century; length of kit 55cm (21¾in).

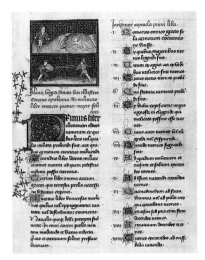

1. *Page from Frontinus 'Strategemata', Vegetius 'De Re Militari', manuscript, French, 1498-1515, 34.3 × 25.4cm (13¼ × 10in).*

2. *Gothic Milanese field armour, Italian, c.1450, height c.173cm (68in).*

European Arms and Armour

By far the largest single addition of arms and armour to the Museum was the bequest by Robert Lyons Scott (1871-1939). From 1915 until he died, he was chairman of Scott Shipbuilding and Engineering Co. at Greenock, possibly the oldest shipbuilding company in the world, having been founded in 1711. Scott bought his first flintlock for a few pence when he was a schoolboy, and his interest grew until, at his death, his collection was described as 'one of the choicest ever made in this country or another' and 'the most considerable collection in private hands'. Between 1917 and 1923 Scott took advantage of the fact that the turmoil of World War I caused many to sell their collections and that he was the only British collector with sufficient funds to compete against American millionaires. It was his intention 'to make this collection as representative as possible so that when it became public property it would provide an instructive survey of the history of arms and armour'.

Scott was a worldwide traveller and a keen hunter and sportsman. He was a first-class amateur fencer and represented Scotland in international events. During the last fifteen years of his life he concentrated on creating a superb reference library of over 3000 books dealing with the military sciences, the section on fencing being one of the finest in the world [1], bearing out what was said of the armour and weapons when he died, 'none have had masters better versed in their points than was Mr Scott'.

One of the most impressive objects in the Scott collection is probably the Greenwich armour for man and horse (*c*.1550-1558) [3], the only example of its type to survive. It was a field armour belonging to the 1st Earl of Pembroke, William Herbert (1501?-1570), and was used for battle, possibly against the French at St Quentin in 1557. It was made by the Greenwich Armoury which was set up by Henry VIII to make high quality armour for the royalty and nobility. The armour was described in 1635 as 'richly graven and gilded' and this decoration still exists.

The Gothic Milanese field armour of about 1450 [2] is probably the earliest and most complete plate armour in Britain. Made in Milan by various local armourers, some specializing in the leg pieces, others the arms, and so on, it weighs 26.5 kilograms (58lb 9oz). The armour was proofed, or tested, by firing crossbow bolts at it, and the resulting strike marks can still be seen on the fauld, or laminated skirt. This type of armour was the supreme achievement of the armourer's craft, protective of the body and beautifully formed. Scott bought it in 1938 from the American newspaper magnate, William Randolph Hearst, and its excellent state of preservation is due to the fact that until the mid-1930s, when Hearst bought it, it was at the armoury of Churburg Castle in the South Tyrol. The helmet, a burbut weighing three kilograms (6lb 10oz), is contemporary with the armour but does not belong to it, and it still retains its quilted grass padding. Like other

3. Greenwich field armour for man and horse, English, c.1550-58, height of man's armour 162.5cm (64in).

4. Close helmet with visor, German, c.1560, height 37.4cm (14¾in).

5. Sallet helmet, German, c.1480, height 25.4cm (10in).

6. Tournament tilting helm, English, c.1475- 1500, height 50.8cm (20in).

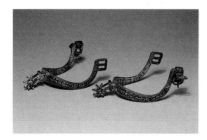

7. *Pair of rowel spurs, German, 16th century, length 12.7cm (5in).*

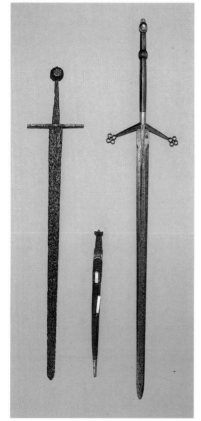

8. *Hand-and-a-half sword, northern European, c.1310-1400; dirk, Scottish, c.1725-1750; claymore, Scottish, c.1550-1560; length of dirk 57.8cm (22¾in).*

pieces of the armour it is stamped with the mark of the armourer who made it.

The German close helmet of about 1560 [4] has a pivoted visor and bevor which allows the front and back parts to pull apart so it can be placed over the head. On the right side of the 'skull' of the helmet is etched the crest of the original owner. Another type of helmet is the German sallet of *c.*1480 [5]. It is probably from Nuremberg and was made from a single piece of metal which would originally have had a bright surface.

A rare English piece is the tilting helm of *c.*1475-1500 [6], which weighs 11.7 kilograms (25lb 13oz). Originally it was thought to be a torture instrument from one of the ships of the Spanish Armada and used by forcing the victim, 'chained upright', to wear it 'and support the weight . . . on his wretched shoulders'. In fact, the reason it was so heavy was to ward off the blows it would receive from opponents in the lists at the tournaments. The hole on its right side, which probably had a door with a spring catch, was for ventilation.

Knights and other horseriders needed spurs, and the pair of 16th-century rowel spurs [7] are a fine example. Scott's spurs form a collection on their own and date from Roman times to the 17th century.

The collection of offensive weapons is also of a very high quality. The hand-and-a-half sword of 1310-1400 [8] is a fine specimen of a medieval sword, with its broad double-edged blade, designed for slashing rather than thrusting. Scott also collected Scottish weapons, as illustrated by the claymore [8] of 1550-60 (the word is anglicized Gaelic for 'great sword'). The dirk [8], a Scottish dagger, was made from the broken blade of a sword by the Birmingham swordmaker W. Harvey, who was active between 1725 and 1750.

The collection of crossbows, an early love of Scott's, includes many major and some early examples, such as the composite crossbow of about 1500 [9]. It has a stock, or tiller, of horn and ivory plaques, and the composite bow, made of layers of horn, wood and glue, is covered with parchment to protect it. Some of Scott's crossbows came from the collection of Sir Ralph Payne-Gallwey, a noted authority on crossbows.

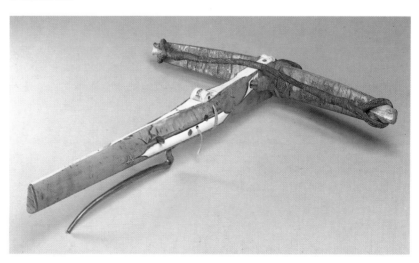

9. *Composite crossbow of horn, wood, ivory and parchment, European, c.1500, length 77.4cm (30½in).*

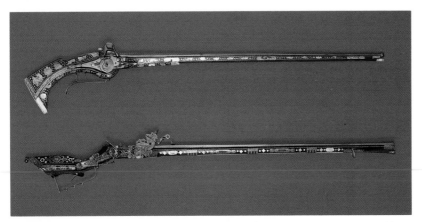

10. *Wheel-lock sporting gun inlaid in ivory and mother-of-pearl, French, c.1600-1610; wheel-lock Tschinke birding rifle, Polish, c.1665; length of rifle 124.5cm (49in).*

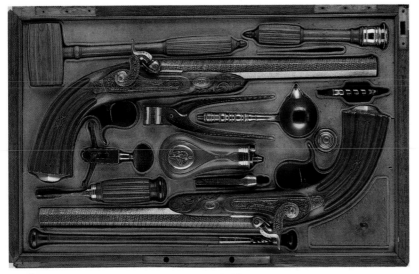

13. *Boxed pair of target pistols by M.J. Chaumont, Belgian, c.1850, size of box 47.6 × 29.2cm (18¾ × 11½in).*

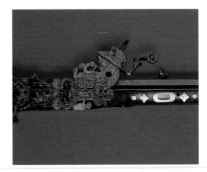

11. *Detail of wheel-lock Tschinke birding rifle.*

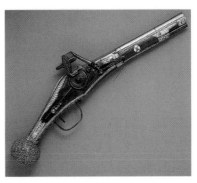

12. *Wheel-lock horseman's pistol inlaid in ivory, German, c.1580-1590, length 51cm (20in).*

12A. *Detail of butt of wheel-lock horseman's pistol.*

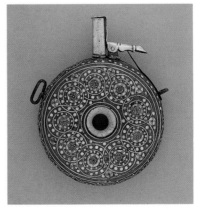

14. *Wooden powder flask inlaid in staghorn and brass, German, 17th century, diameter 12.7cm (5in).*

Scott's hunting interests are reflected in many guns including a wheel-lock sporting gun [10], with fine ivory and mother-of-pearl inlay, and a Tschinke [10] with inlaid gemstones and a brass lock engraved with monkeys [11]. The wheel-lock horseman's pistol [12] also shows intricate ivory inlay, especially on the butt [12A]. Powder for these guns could be carried in powder flasks such as the German priming flask [14] which is of wood inlaid with staghorn and bands and stars of brass.

The pair of boxed single-shot target pistols by M.J. Chaumont of about 1850 [13] represent Liège, a famous centre of Belgian gun manufacturing since the 17th century and still active today. M.J. Chaumont made guns between 1836 and about 1850. More luxurious than normal pocket pistols, these have chiselled furniture and Damascus steel barrels. They were made by welding and twisting several steel rods around a core, giving a striped pattern on the barrel when the rods were welded together and the core removed.

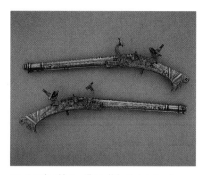

15. *A pair of brass fishtail-butt dags by James Low, Scottish, 1624 and 1626, length of pistols 43.8cm (17¼in).*

The second largest collection of weapons is that of Charles Edward Whitelaw (1869-1939), who began collecting at the age of sixteen when he was given a pistol. He carried on with this interest throughout his life, becoming an authority on Scottish weapons and publishing important papers on basket-hilted swords, Scottish guns and dirks. In 1911 he arranged the Arms and Weapons section of the Historical Exhibition in Glasgow and wrote entries for the accompanying catalogue. It was Whitelaw who was responsible for identifying many of the makers of his weapons, and in 1922 *European Hand Firearms* by H.J. Jackson included a treatise on Scottish firearms by him. In 1936 Whitelaw decided to bequeath part of his collection to the Museum and in 1937 the weapons were given on loan. Before his death in 1939 he had been working on a comprehensive survey of Scottish arms, weapons and their makers which was completed by a librarian at the Tower of London.

The variety of Scottish weapons Whitelaw collected can be demonstrated by several pieces. A pair of all-brass dags, or pistols [15], probably by James Low of Dundee and dated 1624 on the locks and 1626 on the barrels, have stocks and barrels covered with engraved floral and leaf scrolls. A flintlock pistol by Daniel Walker of Dumbarton [16], of about 1700-25, although an example by a 'country' gun maker, is inlaid with engraved silver. Powder for these guns would possibly have been carried in a powder horn such as the example made of flattened cowhorn [16]. The flat surfaces are engraved with interlaced designs and incorporate the initials A.G. and I.D.

The backsword [17], a single-edged blade by Walter Allan of Stirling, is an example of the type of sword made in the early 18th century and is signed W.A. over S. under the backguard. A double-edged broadsword by John Simpson I of Glasgow [17] is inscribed *Gott bewahr die aufrechte Schotten*, 'God protect the upright Scots', and is of the late 17th century.

The targe [17] was also part of the Scottish armoury. This type of shield, made of two-ply wood, had a front covered with tooled leather and a back covered with deer skin. Dating from the early 18th century, this targe was perforated in the centre for a long spike, but this has now been plugged with a brass finial.

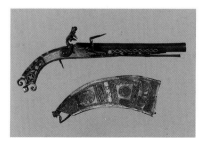

16. *A flintlock pistol by Daniel Walker, Scottish, c.1700-1725, length 40.6cm (16in); engraved cowhorn powder horn, Scottish, early 18th century.*

17. *Single-edged backsword, Scottish, early 18th century; double-edged broadsword, Scottish, late 17th century; Highland targe of wood, leather and deerskin, Scottish, early 18th century; length of broadsword 99cm (39in).*

18. *Experimental target rifle signed by Alexander Henry, Scottish, 1871, length 138.4cm (54½in); Martini-Henry rifle No. 1, British, 1872; length 124.5cm (49in).*

19. *Detail of marks on basket-hilted broadsword.*

The Martin Collection of firearms was on loan to the Museum from 1951 and was bought in 1956 from Alexander E. Martin. The Martin family made fishing rods and tackle, guns and rifles since before 1831 at 20 Exchange Square, Glasgow, and had branches in Aberdeen, Edinburgh and Stirling. Alexander Martin was a well-known international shot, and the collection consisted of 115 firearms including the Henry experimental rifle [18]. This was a muzzle loader made by Alexander Henry (1818-1894) of Edinburgh and London for a competition to find a new barrel to be used in a military breechloading rifle. The search lasted for three years and in 1871 the Henry barrel was chosen and combined with a winning design for the breech by Friedrich Von Martini (1833-1897). The rifle became known as the Martini-Henry rifle, and the first production model, dated 1872, was presented to Henry as a gift [18]. The interior of the steel barrel is rifled, or spirally grooved, to spin the bullet for greater accuracy over distances, and it has a calibre of .450. The stock is of Italian walnut. The rifle was the best of its time, combining a great speed of fire and accuracy (55 rounds in three minutes). The model remained in military use until 1896 when it was superseded by the Lee-Metford.

Charles C.S. Parsons, who lived in Greenock near R.L. Scott, had a major interest in European edged weapons, and his collection of 205 items was bought in 1911. Parsons bought pieces not only from dealers but from Scott, Whitelaw and Martin as well. One of his earliest pieces is a North European early 14th-century double-edged broadsword [20]. Running nearly its full length it has a fuller, a groove which reduces the weight of the blade but not its strength. The collection also includes Scottish items, such as a broadsword of the late 17th century, with a pierced basket hilt [20]. The blade bears armourers' marks including a crowned head, repeated [19]. Blades such as these were made in Germany and imported to Scotland where they were married to the Scottish-made hilts. The 14th or 15th-century ballock dagger [20], so called because of the shape of the haunches at the base of the grip, was a medieval precursor to the Scottish dirk. Perhaps French, this piece has an oak grip and iron pommel. Two bands of brass are inserted at the termination of the haunches.

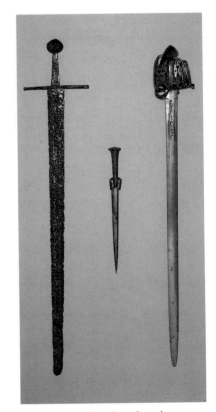

20. *Double-edged broadsword, northern European, 14th century; ballock dagger, French?, 14th or 15th century; basket-hilted broadsword, Scottish, late 17th century; length of dagger 39cm (15⅜in).*

21. Company Sergeant-Major's full dress uniform, 1st Lanarkshire Engineer Volunteers, 1883-1908; Other Ranks helmet, 1901-1908.

Militaria

In 1975 the Museum purchased the collection of over two hundred uniforms, badges and books belonging to Captain Philippe Durand (1879-1976), and these form the major part of the Museum's own collection. Captain Durand joined the Royal Artillery in 1897 and served until 1912. In 1914 he re-enlisted, serving until 1920, at which time he was in the Highland Light Infantry.

Amongst many others, Captain Durand had two major interests, philately and militaria, and his military background led him to develop his deep interest in badges and uniforms, many of which he bought in the Barrows Market in Glasgow. Between 1923 and 1954 he was curator of the People's Palace, Glasgow, where his collection of uniforms was often on display. After his retirement he became honorary curator of Provand's Lordship. During the 1920s he founded *Badge Collectors Quarterly*, a journal which lasted until the late 1950s.

The Company Sergeant-Major's full dress tunic of the 1st Lanarkshire Engineer Volunteers, which dates from between 1883 and 1908 [21] is an interesting example from his collection. This regiment was formed in 1863 from the 1st, 2nd and 3rd Lanarkshire Engineers of the 97th Lanarkshire Rifle Volunteers and retained a spike on their helmet when other regiments substituted a ball. This can be seen clearly on the Other Ranks helmet [21], which dates from 1901 to 1908 and bears the Regimental badge of white metal with the King's crown.

Medals

The medals won by Colour Sergeant Henry McDonald (1823-1893) of the Royal Engineers during the Crimean War (1853-1856) were donated in 1968 and form a collection in themselves.

During the Crimean War, the Russian troops fortified the naval port of Sevastopol against the opposing Allied troops consisting of British, French and Turkish forces. Amongst the fortifications was the Mamelon, a hill surmounted by a tower in front of which the Russians had dug rifle pits. On 19 April 1855 the British made an assault on these pits. McDonald won his V.C. in this engagement, when in an attempt on the pits two officers were disabled 'and command devolved upon him, and he determinately persisted in carrying on the sap, withstanding the repeated attacks of the enemy'. Although wounded, McDonald successfully effected a 'lodgement' in the enemies' rifle pits. He was twice mentioned in dispatches but retired from the army at a comparatively early age, one of only eight Royal Engineers to win the V.C. during the Crimean War.

McDonald's medals [22] include the Victoria Cross, which is awarded for valour and is the highest decoration that can be won by a member of the armed forces of Britain or Commonwealth countries; the Distinguished Conduct Medal, which is earned for meritorious service; the Crimean Medal (with three clasps for the battles of Alma, Inkerman and Sevastopol) which was given to those who took part in the conflict; and the French *Légion d'Honneur*, which is presented for distinguished military services.

22. Group of medals awarded to Colour Sergeant Henry McDonald V.C.: the Victoria Cross; the Distinguished Conduct Medal; the Crimean Medal; the Légion d'Honneur.

Decorative Art

Introduction

The Department of Decorative Art at Kelvingrove was established in 1973 by the then Director, Trevor Walden. This was almost one hundred years after the first of the objects now under its care came to Glasgow's growing museum collections. That last quarter of the 19th century saw the emergence of the idea that the market was in danger of being swamped by the sheer quantity of products being made available by means of mass production. Several writers, educators and industrialists of the time accepted the idea that quality was equally important, that the application of 'art' to 'industry' was a desirable goal; and many felt that museums had a vital role to play in this by showing the general public the best of past and present production, whether they were common or garden household wares or fine metalwork or textiles. The applied or decorative art collections of most national or civic museums have their origins in this concept although its application has perhaps at times been haphazard.

The Department comprises important collections of metalwork, ceramics, glass, furniture, costume and textiles, although not all were represented in the early stages of its growth, and only the first three of the groups are now actually housed at the Art Gallery and Museum. Over the years, collecting policies have been developed, changes of emphasis have occurred and chance has played a significant role in shaping present activities.

During the 1880s and 1890s the collections were developed largely through purchase. Dealers, private collectors and auction houses, both at home and abroad, provided examples of Western European and Oriental art to demonstrate to the people of Glasgow the achievements of past and contemporary craftsmen. Glasgow manufacturers were a vital part of the plan. Their products formed the basis of displays on how things were made — an invaluable aid to the appreciation of any object. In this way, particularly from some of the spectacular sales such as those of the Spitzer Collection in Paris in 1893 or the Hamilton Palace collections in London in 1882, came many of the finest items of ceramic and glass. The aim was to build up a representative collection of historic and modern material. At the same time many private people in the city were starting their own collections — Sir William Burrell, J.A. Fleming and many others. Over the next forty years they must have known about each other's interests as well as those of the Museum. All or part of many of these collections were later gifted to the Museum, and rarely is there any duplication of material.

The ceramic collections have grown steadily since the early days, initially by a combination of purchases from factories, especially from art potters such as Elton, Ruskin and della Robbia, and of small gifts. This growth was relatively slow, but the size and scope of the collec-

Tin-glazed earthenware bottle from the Delftfield Pottery, Glasgow.

tions were increased enormously by the gift of over 600 items of ceramics and glass by Miss A. Fleming in 1938 and three years later by Victor J. Cumming's Gift in memory of his mother of 475 items, mostly of English porcelain. The Fleming Gift added a particular Scottish dimension to the collections at Kelvingrove (the 'Old Glasgow Museum' at the People's Palace had been acquiring local material for some time), and this was reinforced in 1937 by the Cochran Bequest. Robert Cochran gave early Victorian Glasgow wares, and afterwards his sister, Lady Ross Taylor, added more, similar material which had been collected in the 1870s. In the postwar era, a major group of ceramic material was bequeathed by R.H. Lennox. The pieces had been inherited by him as a descendant of the company manager, William Young, of the Delftfield Company of Glasgow and illustrate its last years.

Recent years have seen a consolidation of the collections and an emphasis on areas where the collection is already important — tin-glazed earthenwares, Scottish ceramics of all types and studio ceramics. Few contemporary collectors can afford to give away their collections, and aquisitions are again the mixture of purchases and smaller gifts that was the pattern over a century ago.

The glass collections have developed in a similar manner, although some of the early collections, particularly from Glasgow makers, have been lost, either due to changes in curatorial attitude or because of the damage sustained by the building when a land mine was dropped on the bank of the River Kelvin in March 1941. Three major collections are of particular note. All but half a dozen items of Spanish glass came from one of Spain's great connoisseurs of the subject, Juan de Riaño. The British glass collections are based on generous gifts by Victor Cumming of early 19th-century Scottish glassware but more particularly on nearly two hundred items from Miss J.C.C. Macdonald in 1947. This latter collection included examples of most types of 18th and 19th-century drinking glasses — wines, ales, firing glasses, rummers, over thirty 'thistle' glasses of various types and an important group of Bohemian glass.

J.A. Fleming.

The Cumming Collection in situ *at 8 Grosvenor Terrace.*

James Paton, Superintendent at Glasgow Art Gallery & Museum 1876-1914, founder of the Decorative Art collections, by Joseph Henderson.

More recently, emphasis has been on the acquisition of finest quality items to fill gaps in the collection and on a considerable expansion of the number of pieces of Scottish contemporary glass. As with the ceramics, only a very small part of the collection can be displayed because of lack of space.

The metalwork collections, mostly of silver, have developed in a rather haphazard manner. In the latter years of the last century, Elkington plate reproductions of important historic pieces, mostly in the Victoria and Albert Museum in London, were purchased. It was a common practice in civic museums at that time to use replicas to a much greater extent than is now the case. Some years later, in 1903, an important collection of Scandinavian silver was purchased specifically to enhance the holdings of traditional crafts. Over the next thirty years only individual pieces came into the collection. There does not appear to have been any definite collecting policy in this period, although this apparent inactivity may well have been the result of the knowledge that two of Glasgow's greatest private collectors were active in the same field at the time — Sir William Burrell and Victor J. Cumming.

Cumming was inward freight manager for the Donaldson Line for fifty years and a member of the Trades House and the Old Glasgow Club. His mother, Helen Cumming, an ardent collector of ceramics, had encouraged her son to collect and he specialized in silver after 1700, particularly Scottish silver. Sir William Burrell's collection, on the other hand, contains few items after 1700 and virtually no Scottish material, and it seems probable that the Museum's directorate was aware that both collections would eventually be given to the City.

The Cumming Collection was exhibited at the Art Gallery in 1945 and given to the museum the following year (Sir William Burrell had formally given his collection in 1944). Almost overnight, therefore, the City could boast a representative collection of silver, and Kelvingrove a particularly strong collection of Scottish silver. From that time there has been a well-defined policy of collecting Scottish, and particularly West of Scotland silver, and representative British pieces for comparison.

Another very specific collection of silverware is also now in the care of the Department, namely the racing trophies of one of Glasgow's most famous sons, Sir Thomas Lipton. Originally presented to the People's Palace (the Old Glasgow Museum) in 1932, his trophies and other memorabilia were moved to Kelvingrove in the 1970s.

As the newest of the Museum's curatorial sections in an already overcrowded building, there is little space available for Decorative Art to show the full range of its collections. The costume and textile collection is housed at Camphill House, while most of the furniture collection remains in store, shown only in temporary exhibitions or in the Glasgow Style Gallery. The Department owes its existence to two of Glasgow's most dynamic directors and continues with a policy of collecting and displaying the range and quality of Scottish craftsmanship from the 17th century to the present day in the fields of ceramics, glass, metalwork, woodwork and costume in their British and European context.

Silver

Glasgow

Glasgow's silver collection includes wares made in towns as far apart as Aberdeen and Calcutta. At the heart is the large and comprehensive group made in Glasgow itself, dating from the late 17th century until the 1930s, with emphasis on the 18th and early 19th centuries. Each piece is stamped with the maker's mark and most bear the town mark, indicating that the silver is of the correct purity — an early form of consumer protection. Glasgow's town mark [1] is complex, with the oak tree, the bird, bell and salmon with a gold ring in its mouth associated with the legend of St Mungo, the city's patron, portrayed on the city's coat of arms.

Although silversmiths are known to have served the local population, both ecclesiastical and secular, for centuries, few pieces survive until well into the 17th century. The tiny filigree patchbox by William Clerk [2], dating from about 1695, is our earliest example of a local silversmith's craft. Typical of most Scottish silver of the period, the delicate patchbox has more in common with European and Scandinavian silver than with English precedents, hardly surprising given Scotland's troubled political relations with England at that time and the strong trading links with the rest of Europe.

Glasgow silversmithing in the 18th century was dominated numerically by the Luke family, with six members of it working in the city from the late 17th century until the 1750s. Other notable 18th-century smiths were Adam Graham, Johan Gotlieff Bilsinds, James Glen, Robert Gray and the firm of Milne & Campbell. Their work illustrates the gradual development of 18th-century domestic silver,

1. *Town mark for Glasgow silver.*

2. *Filigree patchbox by William Clerk, Glasgow, c.1695, 3.8cm (1½in) diameter.*

3. *18th-century Glasgow domestic silver: two caddies, two chocolate pots, two teapots and a sugar basin; diameter of basin 12.4cm (4⅞in).*

4. *Communion cup by John Luke, Glasgow, c.1700, height 19.1cm (7½in).*

from thistle mugs and quaichs to tea and chocolate pots, tea caddies and sugar basins, salvers and waiters, sauce boats, condiments and cutlery [3, 7]. The thistle mug and quaich — a shallow drinking vessel, large or small, with flat handles — are peculiarly Scottish forms. Locally made plate for use in communion services ranges in date from John Luke's cup of about 1700 [4], made for the parish of Cardross, to pieces from the early 20th century.

As the 18th century progressed, local smiths looked increasingly towards London although their work still retained a distinctively Scottish appearance: well-balanced shapes made from a satisfying thickness of metal, usually with minimal decoration. Weighty and practical, this domestic silver would have been a delight to use.

Glasgow silversmiths seemed especially happy with the more sculptural and naturalistic forms of the early 19th century. One fine example is the two-handled cup and cover by Robert Gray & Son [8], presented by the Glasgow Goldsmiths Company to Kirkman Finlay in thanks for his 'exertions' on their behalf in the establishment of an assay office in the city in 1819. Later 19th and early 20th-century silver is not well represented in the collection. Many of the cheaper silver wares may have been made in the manufacturing centres of Sheffield and Birmingham and sent to assay in Glasgow, perhaps because Scottish customers preferred a local hallmark. Nevertheless, Glasgow silversmiths were exploiting exotic themes, like the Indian zodiac pattern registered by James Reid & Co. in 1878 [5]. Their work could also be of supreme quality, as in the finely modelled plaques on the Edinburgh Gold Cup of 1902 [6], hallmarked by Smith & Rait of Glasgow. The most amusing piece of local plate is a three dimensional representation of the City's coat of arms in silver-gilt, fashioned as a table lamp by Edward & Sons in 1937.

5. *Detail of Indian pattern teapot by James Reid & Co., Glasgow, 1878, height 24.4cm (9¾in).*

6. *Gold Cup for Edinburgh Races by Smith & Rait, Glasgow, 1902, length 36.7cm (14½in).*

7. *18th-century Glasgow domestic silver: two mugs, salt, small quaich, tankard, large quaich, two thistle mugs and a sauceboat; diameter of large quaich 18.4cm (7¼in).*

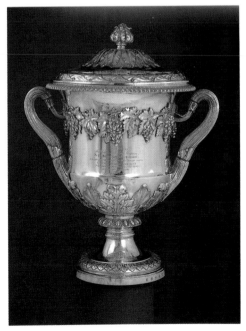

8. *Two-handled cup and cover by Robert Gray & Son, Glasgow, c.1820, height 38.9cm (15½in).*

Edinburgh and the Scottish Burghs

Some of the finest quality silver made in Scotland was hallmarked by Edinburgh silversmiths. During the 18th century, in particular, Edinburgh makers produced pieces of the highest fashion, capable of rivalling those of the London makers. Glasgow has a representative collection of 18th-century Edinburgh-made domestic silver, with only a few items dating from earlier or later.

Edinburgh was established as the first assaying authority in Scotland; today it has Scotland's only assay office, the Glasgow office having closed in 1964. Since 1485 Edinburgh silver has been stamped with its town mark of the triple towered castle. The earliest example of Edinburgh silver in the collection is also our earliest piece of Scottish silver: a communion cup from a set of four made by Patrick Borthwick for the parish of Haddington, dated 1645 by the inscription [9]. With its hexagonal foot and bands of decoration this fine cup has much in common with contemporary European silver.

In 1687 the Edinburgh goldsmiths were granted a charter by King James VII and II, extending their supervisory powers throughout Scotland. Edinburgh goldsmiths were authorized to make unannounced visits to distant burghs in order to test or assay the wares in the silversmiths' workshops for the purity of the silver. Until then, isolated craftsmen had been trusted, without official checks, not to lower the quality of their metal by adding further quantities of base metal to the alloy. Wares were stamped with the maker's initials and the town mark, usually derived from the burgh arms, such as Aberdeen [10], Arbroath, Dundee, Greenock, Montrose, Perth and St Andrews, or the town's full name, if short enough, for example, Tain, Wick and Elgin. This continued until 1836 when all smiths were obliged to have their wares assayed in Edinburgh or Glasgow.

Flatware — ladles and spoons in amazing variety [11] — and small domestic wares were the main products of the burgh smiths, many of whom are represented in the collection. Their work is characterized by strong, simple lines and excellent working proportions.

9. *Communion cup by Patrick Borthwick, Edinburgh, c.1645, height 33cm (13in).*

10. *Cross-belt plate of the 3rd Regiment Aberdeenshire Local Militia by J. Erskine, Aberdeen, c.1808/9, height 8.1cm (3¼in).*

11. *18th-century Scottish flatware: teaspoons, dessert spoons, tablespoons and ladles; length of teaspoons 12cm (4¾in).*

London

London-made silver has been the fashion leader in England throughout the centuries, and in Scotland from about 1700. Since 1300, hallmarking has exercised quality control over the wares of London smiths and continues today; silversmithing has always been a highly organized craft catering for a sophisticated market.

12. *Coffee pot by Daniel Garnier, c.1710; sugar basin with cover by Ralph Maidman, 1733, London; height of pot 23.8cm (9¼in).*

13. *Tea urn by Hester Bateman, London, 1780, height 55cm (21⅝in).*

14. *Box by Alexander Johnston, London, 1759, width 9.8cm (3¾in).*

15. *Silver-gilt bowl and cover designed by William Beckford, made by Paul Storr, London, 1813, diameter 11.2cm (4⅜in).*

Glasgow's collection of London-made plate is generally after 1700 in date, in contrast to the group purchased by Sir William Burrell, on display in the Burrell Collection, which is mainly from the earlier period. Most is domestic silver — candlesticks, salvers, spoons, argylls (heated sauceboats), baskets, sugar bowls, tea vases, milk jugs [12] — illustrating the stylistic development of London silver from the simple geometric lines of the early 18th century through the ebullient chased decoration of the Rococo [14] and the balanced neoclassical [13] forms favoured towards the end of the century to the more sculptural forms of the early 19th century. Paul Storr, the best known of the Regency craftsmen, is represented by a fine group of domestic and presentation plate. His mark is also on the set of four delightful and idiosyncratic silver-gilt preserve dishes made for William Beckford of Fonthill, a noted connoisseur and collector, to his own design in 1813 [15].

Victorian and Edwardian plate is seen at its most exuberant in the large collection of trophies presented by Sir Thomas Lipton. Similar in date but in complete contrast stylistically is the small group of wares by English silversmiths who were influenced by the Arts and Crafts movement. One piece of the highest quality is a green glass decanter by Charles Ashbee's Guild of Handicraft dated 1901, on loan to the museum.

Presentations and Testimonials

Silver and gold are the traditional materials for formal gifts and awards. Glasgow is lucky to have an interesting group of these tangible forms of gratitude and respect, honouring both national celebrity and local service. An example of the latter is a plate presented to the Reverend John Burns, minister of the Barony Church in 1826 [19]. West of Scotland men whose worth was recognized outwith their home and commemorated in trophies now in Kelvingrove include Patrick Colquhoun and Sir Colin Campbell. Patrick Colquhoun (1745-1820), a businessman of the highest calibre with a strong and practical social conscience, was, or at least his wife was, presented in 1785 with a tea urn and tray by the 'Manufacturers of Muslins . . . in the City of Glasgow'. In 1840 Sir Colin Campbell, Baron Clyde (1792-1863), the famous career soldier, was presented with a silver replica of the Warwick Vase [16] by the citizens of Halifax, Nova Scotia, whose lieutenant-governor he had been for six years. The original Warwick Vase, a popular model for such smaller trophies, is now in Glasgow, at the Burrell Collection.

In 1937, Sir Thomas Lipton, the famous grocer and dedicated competitive sailor, bequeathed his lifelong collection of presentation plate and sailing trophies to Glasgow, his home city. Most are typical in scale and decoration of later Victorian and early Edwardian plate. Especially impressive is a massive punch bowl on its own stand, accompanied by eleven goblets and a ladle, which was made by Tiffany & Co. of New York as a sailing trophy and won by Sir Thomas in 1902. In 1930, after his fifth unsuccessful attempt to regain the America's Cup for Britain, Lipton — 'the Gamest loser in the World of Sport' — was presented with a gold two-handled cup and cover [17] by the American people, a 'symbol of a voluntary outpouring of Love, Admiration and Esteem'.

One trophy which, perhaps surprisingly, has found a home in Glasgow is the silver two-handled cup presented to John Philip Kemble (1757-1823), the renowned actor, on his retirement from the stage in June 1823. Certainly the most touching trophy is the silver-gilt two-handled cup made by Paul Storr [18] which was given by William Beckford 'to his dear Grandchild and Godson William Alexander Anthony Archibald Earl of Angus and Arran on the 18 February 1812 the first Anniversary of his Birth'.

16. Silver replica of the Warwick Vase by Barnard Bros., London, 1840, height 66.5cm (26¼in).

17. Two-handled gold cup and cover by Tiffany & Co., New York, 1930, height 44.4cm (17½in).

19. Detail from presentation plate by Mitchell & Son and R. Gray, Glasgow, 1826, diameter 37.7cm (14⅞in).

18. Silver-gilt two handled cup by Paul Storr, London, 1809, height 9.5cm (3¾in).

Scandinavian and Colonial

Two of the more unusual groups of silver in the collections come from the Scandinavian countries and from the former British colonies.

The Scandinavian silver includes pieces from Norway, Denmark and Sweden. It was bought in 1902 and 1903 with assistance from the Board of Education, the intention being to show the traditional crafts of the world to the local population and to the students of design at the Glasgow School of Art. Consequently, traditional folk forms are well represented, such as tankards [22], beakers, wine tasters, buckles and clasps, and spoons of myriad variety [20], all dating from the 17th until the 19th centuries. None of the domestic plate of the same period was purchased as it was considered to have no relevance to traditional Scandinavian plate and therefore to be of no educational value.

20. *Silver spoons, Scandinavian, 17th and 18th centuries, length 18.9cm (7⅜in).*

21. *Salt and pepper by William Henry Twentyman, Calcutta, early 19th century, height 9.5cm (3¾in).*

22. *Tankard by Jochim Kirsebom, Stavanger, Norway, c.1623, height 23cm (9in).*

When the Indian, Jamaican and Maltese teapots, sugar bowls, salvers, condiments and pans were given to the Museum, their confusing marks were interpreted as those of Inverness, Aberdeen and Edinburgh Canongate. However, later research has shown that in the late 18th and early 19th centuries when silver was made by expatriate silversmiths for expatriate patrons, customers expected their silverware to have hallmarks, hence the misleading groups of makers' initials, animals and thistles. Today, we recognize that this silver, such as Indian silver from Calcutta and Madras [21], has little in common with the work of contemporary Scottish smiths.

Jewellery

The jewellery collection was the gift of Mrs Anne and Professor John Hull Grundy between 1975 and 1984. The pieces range in date from the early 18th century to the 1930s, the emphasis being on the colourful 'Scottish' jewellery [1] so popular in the 19th century and in the Arts and Crafts and Art Nouveau pieces of the late 19th and early 20th centuries.

Jewellery of the 18th and early 19th centuries forms a small but attractive group. Materials include cut steel and cast iron, called Berlin Iron [2], paste or glass [3], gems [4], coloured and textured gold [5], enamel decoration and carved and tinted ivory [8]. Common to all is a repertory of motifs drawn from nature, a theme which remained popular throughout the 19th century. Technical precision and delicacy of treatment on a tiny scale are typical, with some of the most exquisite craftsmanship seen in the French and English coloured and textured gold.

Victorian jewellery in all its many forms is well represented in the Hull Grundy Gift, illustrating the expanding markets, ever-widening horizons and ceaseless technological advance which characterized the century. Improved communications and travel — Thomas Cook organized his first Continental tour in 1856 — and the many international exhibitions throughout Britain fostered a growing interest in distant lands and alien cultures. Souvenirs arrived in abundance: mosaics [6], cameos and coral [7] from Italy; carved ivory from Switzerland; even elephant-hair bangles from India. Increasing antiquarian study produced 'archaeological' jewellery — reproductions of ancient or historic forms and of ancient techniques, such as gold granulation [9].

All things Scottish were especially popular in the 19th-century, a fashioned encouraged by Queen Victoria. The 'Scottish' jewellery includes re-interpretations of traditional Celtic forms and pebble settings [10, 11] in amazing variety. Some pieces were made in Scotland, usually of subtly hued granite laid in silver. The majority of the more brightly coloured examples, including novelties like bagpipes and barred-gate brooches as well as the ever-popular butterflies [14] and arrows, may have been made in major industrial centres such as Birmingham or Sheffield, the agates, jasper and cornelian having been prepared in Germany.

Mourning and commemorative [12, 13] jewellery, of black enamel on gold set with pearl 'tears', of carved jet, black glass or French jet and vulcanite, or of woven and plaited human hair, forms an extraordinary and distinctively Victorian group. Queen Victoria's adherence to full mourning for the remainder of her long reign after Prince Albert's death in 1861 encouraged all her subjects to follow suit.

Towards the end of the 19th century the market diverged with customers demanding widely differing styles of jewellery. The manufacturing centres produced quantities of often charming stamped silver novelties, usually for the cheaper end of the market — brooches engraved with 'Mother' or 'Baby', sporting pins, souvenirs of the

4. Brooch of foil-backed garnets, English, c.1740, length 9.7cm (3¾in).

2. Berlin iron buckle, German, c.1815; pinchbeck and cut steel buckles, English, early 19th century; length of buckles 4.2cm (1¼in).

1. Paste stones and gold thistle brooch, English, c.1820, length 3cm (1¼in).

3. 'Vauxhall' glass and gold metal insect brooch, English, early 19th century, length 4.3cm (1¾in).

5. Textured gold and tinted ivory brooch, English?, c.1840, length 4.3cm (1¾in).

6. *Gold metal and Italian stone mosaic cockerel brooch, late 19th century, length 5.7cm (2¼in).*

7. *Coral bracelet and brooch, English, mid-19th century, length of brooch 5.6cm (2¼in).*

8. *Blue glass and ivory ship pendant/brooch, European, possibly French, late 18th-early 19th century, length 2.8cm (1⅛in).*

9. *Gold ram's head brooch by Castellani, Italian, 19th century, length 3cm (1⅛in).*

10. *Gilt metal, pebblestone and paste stone buckle, English, c.1870, length 7.4cm (3in).*

11. *Silver and pebblestone star-shaped brooch and bar brooch, Scottish, mid-19th century, length of bar brooch 8.4cm (3¼in).*

12. *Gold and enamel mourning pendant, British, c.1807, height 4.1cm (1¾in).*

13. *Italian cameo within English setting, 19th century, height 5.1cm (2in).*

14. *Moss agate and gold metal butterfly brooch, English, early 19th century, width 5.8cm (2¼in).*

15. *Art Nouveau waist buckles, left French, right English, 1906, width of French buckle 6cm (2⅜in).*

16. *Corsage brooch of amethyst-coloured paste and gold by James Cromer Watt, Scottish, c.1900, height 10cm (4in).*

17. *Tortoiseshell haircomb, top in silver and gold metal with moonstones and enamel, roundels by Henry Wilson, English, c.1900, width 7cm (2¾in).*

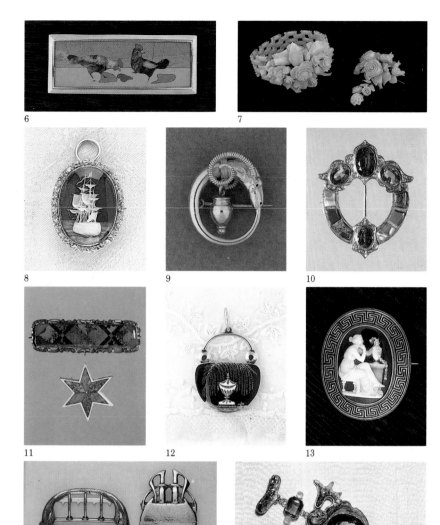

6 7 8 9 10 11 12 13 15 16

14

17

1887 Jubilee, and many more. Austere and delicate gold and platinum mounts set with pearls or open-backed gems catered for the wealthier customer. Arts and Crafts jewellery, made by hand of non-precious materials such as pastes [16], horn, tortoiseshell, mother-of-pearl, pewter, earthenware and glass, was a reaction against a perceived overabundance of jewellery made by machine. One of Kelvingrove's finest pieces, a *plique-à-jour* (stained-glass technique) enamel and silver haircomb by Henry Wilson [17], is an exceptional example of Arts and Crafts jewellery.

Jewellery in the Art Nouveau style — buckles [15], pendants, hatpins, brooches and haircombs — dating from between 1890 and 1910, forms a major group. Many of the best-known commercial firms are represented, including Celtic-inspired interwoven patterns from Liberty of London and the sinuous curves of the Continental and American designers. Silver was the favourite material, often with enamel decoration in a limited range of colours.

Furniture and Interiors

For many years the furniture collection developed in a haphazard fashion through a series of gifts and bequests and some purchases. Most of the material acquired in this way was 19th century in date and of uneven quality, ranging from a folding footstool to a chair designed by Carlo Bugatti [1], father of the motorcar designer, Ettore, which when it was purchased was thought to be Indian. The aim in recent years has been to consolidate the collection concentrating particularly on Scottish furniture and on 20th-century material.

Apart from the furniture and interiors in the Glasgow Style Gallery (see overleaf), there are items drawn from the reserve collection on display in the gallery of 19th-century British painting. These represent some of the numerous themes of Victorian taste, from reproduction of historical styles [2, 5] and mementoes of time spent on the Continent [3, 4] to examples of 'reformed' or 'progressive' furniture [6] from designers like Christopher Dresser and Bruce Talbert, both of whom had Glasgow connections and who repudiated the overblown naturalistic ornament and historicism so dear to most Victorians.

Examples of Scottish furniture of the 18th, 19th and early 20th centuries are displayed in the more appropriate setting of Pollok House, a mid-18th-century mansion with Edwardian additions, presented to the City by Mrs Anne Maxwell Macdonald in 1966.

1. Chair designed by Carlo Bugatti, Italian, c.1895, height 130cm (51in).

2. Secretaire in Louis XVI style, British, late 19th century, height 140cm (55in).

3. *Table top of Florentine mosaic* (pietre dure), *Italian, 1820s, 40 × 54cm (15¼ × 21¼in).*

4. *Table with Florentine mosaic* (pietre dure) *top, Scottish, 1820s, height 83cm (32¼in).*

5. *'Rebel' chair in beech and stamped leather, Scottish, c.1870, height 90cm (35½in).*

6. *Cast-iron chair made at Coalbrookdale and designed by Christopher Dresser, British, 1871, height 134cm (52¾in).*

The Glasgow Style

One of the ground floor galleries is devoted to the work of Charles Rennie Mackintosh (1868-1928) and his contemporaries, who created the Glasgow Style at the turn of the century — a period of intense artistic activity in the city. Mackintosh is represented primarily by his work for Miss Cranston's chain of Tea Rooms in the city. The reconstruction of the startlingly blue Chinese Room [4], removed from her premises in Ingram Street, can be seen as a refined and final statement of the Style, and was Mackintosh's last major furnishing commission before he left Glasgow for Walberswick in Suffolk in 1914.

Another designer championed by Miss Cranston, who went on to achieve international fame, was George Walton (1867-1933). Like many others in Glasgow, he absorbed a love of simple elongated forms and an admiration for the art of Japan from Whistler and his circle [3]. In terms of domestic design, the Glasgow Style proved attractive to those with artistic aspirations among the nouveau riche and professional classes. The elegant and homely drawing room [5] designed by Mackintosh's friend E. A. Taylor (1874-1951) was part of an extensive commission resulting from the Glasgow International Exhibition of 1901; its colour scheme of muted greens and pinks and the use of stylized rose and harebell motifs were characteristic of the Glasgow Style repertoire. The furnishings were manufactured by Wylie & Lochhead, a large and progressive firm which employed many designers, some still in training at the Glasgow School of Art and the Technical College, such as George Logan [2], Jessie King and John Ednie. Other students, many of them women, banded together to form small craft studios throughout the city [1]. Behind all this adventurous design and patronage was the driving force of Fra Newbery, the enlightened Head Master of the Glasgow School of Art.

1. *Vase decorated by E.M. Watt, Scottish, c.1920, height 25cm (9¾in).*

2. *Design for a music room by George Logan, c.1905, 52 × 61cm (20½ × 24in).*

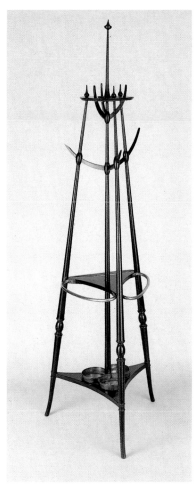

3. *Coat tree from Miss Cranston's Tea Rooms, probably designed by George Walton, 1890s, height 183cm (72in).*

4. *Part of the reconstructed Chinese Tea Room from the Ingram Street Tea Rooms, designed by Charles Rennie Mackintosh, 1911.*

5. *Part of the reconstructed drawing room from the Coats' home at 32 Radnor Road, Handsworth, designed by E.A. Taylor and manufactured by Wylie & Lochhead, 1902.*

Glass

Venice, more particularly the island of Murano, is synonymous with glassmaking, no other European city having such a long continuous tradition of its manufacture. Although small in number, the examples in Glasgow's collections encapsulate the history of glassmaking in the area.

Some thirteen pieces illustrate the golden age of Venetian glass — the 16th century. Featherlight *cristallo* wine glasses, *tazzas* and bowls, and especially a magnificent, clear glass plate [1] with bands of granular gilding, trailed lattimo (white glass) threads, and engraving, of which only five similar examples are known, all demonstrate the skill and technical inventiveness of the early Italian glassmakers.

After a period of decline following a dramatic change in taste during the 18th century and the invasion of Venice by Napoleon in 1797, the industry revived in the 1850s and 60s. The revival was accomplished partly by a detailed study of early forms from Roman to Renaissance, and partly due to a revival of interest in the past. Several companies were established, and these produced copies of various old glasses, which were exhibited at the international exhibitions so popular after 1851. The rest of the collection comprises groups from the Venice and Murano Glass Company [2], purchased from the Paris Exhibition of 1878, and from Salviati and Company [3]. These items include copies of Roman glass and of Renaissance works and 19th-century originals which illustrate the craftsman's joy in working with hot glass.

The Spanish glass collection is the largest in any British museum apart from the Victoria and Albert Museum in London. It was purchased in 1897 from Emilia G. de Riaño, widow of the collector Juan de Riaño, having originally been offered to the Victoria and Albert

1. *Plate of clear glass with gilding, trailed lattimo threads and diamond point engraving, Venetian, 1550-1575, one of only six known examples, diameter 26.5cm (10¼in).*

2. *Wine glass with twisted glass stem, Venetian, c.1878, height 22.6cm (8¾in).*

3. *Centrepiece of light olive glass decorated with dragons and prunts, Venetian, c.1888, diameter 30.5cm (12in).*

4. *Holy water stoup in white, clear and lattimo glass, Castille, Spain, 17th century, height 38.4cm (15⅛in).*

5. *Milk-glass goblet with gilt decoration, Royal Factory of La Granja de San Ildefonso, Spain, 18th century, height 13.7cm (5¾in).*

6. *Clear glass beaker engraved with the arms of the Duke of Medinaceli, Royal Factory of La Granja de San Ildefonso, Spain, 18th century, height 20cm (8¼in).*

7. *Spouted bottle, Persian, 18th century, height 17.7cm (7in).*

which had already purchased over 400 items from de Riaño during his lifetime. It is tantalizing to speculate whether the items now in Glasgow were de Riaño's favourite pieces, ones that he did not wish to sell during his lifetime, or a second collection started after the first had gone to London. Whatever the case, it is undoubtedly representative of Spanish glassmaking from the 16th to 19th centuries.

Spain's peripheral position on the continent of Europe is reflected in her art — the mixing of Arabic and European influence resulting in forms and decoration found nowhere else in Europe. This applies particularly to glass, where the glassmaker seems to have revelled in his mastery of the material. The exuberance of much Spanish glass, particularly that from the southern provinces, is matched only by that of the Venetian glassmakers at their best.

Southern Spanish products are well represented with vases, flasks and bottles from María and Granada in Andalusia. Surprisingly little glass is from Castille, although there is a fine holy water stoup from Cadalso [4]. The largest group is from Catalonia, including an interesting series of specifically Spanish forms — *càntirs* [8], *porons* and *almorratxas*. From Mataró there are two fine pairs of candlesticks. The Royal factory of La Granja de San Ildefonso near Madrid is well represented with both fire-gilt decanters and vases, *façon de Venise* (Venetian-style) and milk glass [5]. Perhaps the most important single item in the collection is the large beaker [6] engraved with the arms of the Duke of Medinaceli, probably by Laurence Eder, the pair to which is in the Museo Arqueologico Nacional, Madrid.

Apart from Venetian and Spanish glass the collections are weak in other European wares. There is a small group of 18th and 19th-century Persian glass [7] which includes elegant swan-necked sprinklers and rich blue bottles.

8. *Group of Spanish glass: vase and toy dove, southern Spanish, 19th century; wine jug (cantir), 18th century; oil and vinegar bottle, 18th century; height of vase 38.5cm (15¼in).*

French glass is poorly represented. Two early 19th-century salts may be French or German and are the only items apart from a few small superb pieces by the great Art Nouveau glass artist Emile Gallé. These represent in miniature the main themes of his work, comprising an important vase [9] with brown glass inlay exquisitely enamelled with hyacinths; a clear glass vase with engraved gilt and enamel decoration of a hunting scene; a rectangular perfume bottle [9] also enamelled; and a vase in the shape of a mosque lamp with enamelled floral ornament.

Central European wares include Bohemian flashed and ruby glass and an interesting group of historical copies by the Rhine Glass Works Company. There are also six examples of Austrian enamelled wares of the 1880s.

A recent acquisition has been a small enamelled tumbler [10] from the Imperial Russian Glass Factory in St Petersburg, now Leningrad, part of a service commissioned by Tsar Nicholas I.

Twentieth century art glass is represented by a small vase [11] from Tiffany & Co. of New York. European pieces of the same period are an impressive Orrefors grey glass vase from Sweden with an engraved stylized nude by Simon Gate, *c.*1928, and an example of Andreas Dirk Copier's Unica glass produced by the Leerdam glassworks near Rotterdam.

The British glass collections are representative of the main strands of development in the 18th and 19th centuries. They contain few items of the highest quality, apart from an important and growing group of Jacobite glasses. Used for drinking toasts of loyalty to Prince Charles Edward Stewart, toasts to his hoped-for victory at Culloden, and after his flight for his imminent return, these glasses are typical of the mid-18th century drinking glass: well-made, elegant and often

10. *Cut crystal tumbler with flashed blue glass shield and enamelled decoration from a service commissioned by Tsar Nicholas I for his summer residence of Alexandria at Peterhof, Imperial Glass Manufactory, St Petersburg (Leningrad), Russian, c.1830, height 7.3cm (2⅞in).*

9. *Perfume bottle in green glass with enamelled and engraved decoration, bowl with enamelled decoration and inlay, by Emile Gallé, French, c.1895, height of bowl 10.2cm (4in).*

11. *Red glass vase by L.C. Tiffany, American, early 20th century, height 7cm (2¾in).*

superbly engraved. Examples in the collection include more common types decorated with a rose and buds but also rarer types such as one engraved with the motto 'Reddi' and an extremely rare 'Amen' glass [13] which carries the Jacobite anthem. Other engraved 18th-century glass includes a fine mammoth goblet, probably from Bristol.

The wide range of different types of British 18th-century wares [14] associated with drinking are represented, from stirrup cups to ale glasses, liquor glasses to decanters, in their variety of forms, including two enamelled by members of the Beilby family of Newcastle. The 19th-century British glass is less impressive as the accent at this point moves towards Scottish-produced glass. There are, however, good examples of early Irish glass and some attractive 'friggers' in the shape of rolling pins, shepherd's crooks and even a glass snake!

After several false starts, the glass industry became established in Scotland during the 19th century. Many of the glasshouses, for example, Verreville in Glasgow, are known only by name or from catalogues — no definitely attributable products survive. The majority of the items in the collections are, however, well provenanced and include most of the types of glass produced in the country. From the early part of the century there are bottles from Dumbarton or Alloa, several bearing 'chip-engraving', a rustic form of decoration practised on wine bottles and often named and dated. In the latter half of the century the industry became firmly established in Glasgow, at the same time as the Art Gallery and Museum was widening its collections. From Couper's and Baird's examples of current production [12] were obtained, either on loan or by gift. Some have since disappeared, but there is an impressive collection of engraved glass from the 1880s as well as a small collection of Clutha glass and samples of other material from Couper's glasshouse.

12. *Decanter and glass with copper-wheel engraving by H. Keller, John Baird Ltd, Glasgow, c.1886, height of decanter 31cm (12¼in).*

13. *The 'Erskine' Amen glass, English, c.1740-1750, height 17.2cm (6¾in).*

14. *Group of English 18th-century drinking glasses showing the variety of shapes of bowl and stem, height of engraved glass 18.5cm (7¼in).*

Edinburgh glasshouses had a higher reputation than those on the west coast, and there is a particularly fine collection of Jenkinson's glass [17], the forerunners of the present-day Edinburgh Crystal, although interestingly the 19th-century wares are largely coloured glass in imitation of Venetian styles. Edinburgh Crystal wares of the 20th century are represented by specimens from the postwar years and today, as are the Monart wares [15] produced by Moncrieff's of Perth in the 1920s and 1930s.

Since the last war there has been a revival of glassmaking in Scotland, and Glasgow boasts the largest collection of contemporary Scottish glass in any museum. The most significant factor in this revival was the establishment of the department of Glass Design at Edinburgh College of Art in the 1940s under Helen Turner. From there students have moved into commercial companies and have set up their own workshops, at first largely as engravers but later also working in hot glass. Herself an engraver, Helen Turner revived one of the oldest forms of decorating glass in Scotland, and the museum has examples of work by those she worked with or trained, from Harold Gordon to Dennis Mann, Alison Geissler, Alison Kinnaird [16] and many

15. *Monart vase, Scottish, c.1930, height 30.5cm (12in).*

16. *Copper-wheel engraved colour-cased crystal plate by Alison Kinnaird with wood and silver mount, Scottish, 1980, diameter 27.4cm (10¾in).*

17. *Cocktail glass by Alexander Jenkinson & Co., Edinburgh, c.1876, height 10cm (4in).*

others. Graduates of the department were closely associated with the establishment of Caithness Glass at Wick, Oban and Perth and with Strathearn Glass at Crieff, two of the most successful modern companies whose wares from ordinary table glass to specially commissioned pieces are well represented.

Scotland has been in the vanguard of the vogue for paperweight making and collecting [18]. The collection includes all types, from the traditional millefiori of Perthshire Paperweights to the abstract design of Colin Terris for Caithness, Peter Holmes of Selkirk Glass, and individual craftsmen such as Peter Layton.

The 'hot-glass' movement of the 1960s inspired many individual craftsmen all over the world, several of whom have settled in Scotland. Ed Iglehart, Frits Akerboom, David Kaplan and many others are represented in the collection, as are the new generation of glassmakers, most of whom trained under John Lawrie [19] at Edinburgh. These include Alison McConachie [20], Anita Pate, Alastair Mackintosh and Sue Murray. The variety of forms, techniques and decorative effects applied to modern glass make this one of the most exciting parts of the collection.

18. *Paperweight by Paul Ysart, Scottish, 20th century, diameter 8.6cm (3⅜in).*

19. *Bosom vase by John Lawrie, Scottish, 1979, height 21cm (8¼in).*

20. *Bowl by Alison McConachie, Scottish, 1985, height 19.5cm (7¾in).*

Ceramics

Glasgow's collection of ceramics is both extensive in scale and comprehensive in scope with well over four thousand items. It reflects the development of European pottery and porcelain from the 16th century to the present day and contains a very wide range of wares.

For a variety of reasons the collection has a particular emphasis upon tin-glazed earthenwares — where tin oxide was used to make the glaze white and opaque — and contains pieces which illustrate the spread of this tradition. A small number of Islamic and Hispano-Moresque items demonstrate the roots of the tradition in Arab culture, and its introduction into Europe through Spain. The most important section, however, is the Italian maiolica, which forms a large and impressive group. The technique of making this type of pottery was taken to Italy from Spain in the 14th century and was developed to a new level of perfection during the Renaissance period [1]. Glasgow's collection contains pieces from most of the principal Italian production centres, dating from the late 15th century to the modern period. It is particularly strong in wares from Castelli, Deruta and Urbino [3], and from the 16th to 18th centuries. The collection began with the acquisition of nine pieces in 1883 and grew with purchases from several important late 19th-century sales. In 1967 the Stirling Maxwell collection, associated with Pollok House, was gifted to the City. This contains some fine maiolica collected in the 1840s and pieces added subsequently. As interest in the ware grew, so in the late 19th century the maiolica tradition was revived in Italy. Some of the best reproductions were made by the Cantagalli family near Florence. In 1899 Glasgow bought fifteen magnificent pieces directly from the makers and these illustrate the fine colours and technical brilliance which can be achieved with this technique [2].

Italian maiolica was admired so much that the technique of making tin-glazed earthenware spread throughout Europe and was developed to create new styles of ware. In France and Germany it is called *faience,* whilst British and Dutch pieces are known as delftware. Glasgow's collection reflects this spread and includes, for example, a large bowl made at Talavera de la Reyna in Spain during the late 17th century [4], which illustrates the developing tradition. Potters in the Netherlands began making tin-glazed earthenwares in the Italian manner early in the 16th century and soon began to evolve a distinctive style of their own. Trade with the east stimulated them to

1. *Spanish tin-glazed earthenware dish with lustre decoration, 17th century?, diameter 28cm (11in).*

2. *Tin-glazed earthenware ewer with painted scene of the Three Wise Men of the East from a Renaissance fresco and a winged caryatid handle, Cantagalli factory, Florence, c.1899, height 72cm (28¼in).*

3. *Italian maiolica wares: salt in the shape of a rabbit, from Castel Durante, c.1600; plate from Urbino, depicting Apollo pursuing Daphne, c.1527; inkstand from Urbino, late 16th century, diameter of plate 26cm (10¼in).*

discover new techniques, and they became particularly skilled at imitating Chinese and Japanese porcelains with their quite different material. Much of their ware, like its Oriental prototypes, was blue and white. These colours are considered typical of Dutch tin-glazed wares which are particularly associated with the town of Delft [5], although delftware was in fact made widely in the Netherlands and a wide range of colours was available. The Dutch pottery industry was at its peak from the mid-17th to mid-18th centuries, and huge quantities of ware were exported and widely copied. The collections contain pieces dating from the 17th century to the 19th, which reflect the significance of this ware.

A more original contribution to the European ceramic heritage came from Germany in the late Middle Ages, where salt-glazed stonewares [6] were developed. These were fired once at a high temperature and then glazed by throwing salt into the kiln to vaporize and transform the surface of the ware. The technique was discovered in the Rhineland, and the ware was made in several places, each of which evolved a characteristic product. The tall white tankards from Sieburg, known as *Schnelles,* are quite different from the grey wares of Raren, decorated with cobalt blue. By the 16th century, a high level had been reached, and salt-glazed wares were exported in large quantities, either as containers for wines or as goods in their own right. There is a small but representative collection of this pottery at Kelvingrove, which does justice to these distinctive wares.

Chinese and Japanese porcelains, which were a quite different material, translucent, white and durable, more than any other ceramic material fascinated Europeans. As soon as regular trade with the Orient began in the 17th century and porcelains became more freely available, attempts to reproduce them were made. At first the material was a complete mystery but at the end of the century some quite convincing artificial or 'soft-paste' porcelains were being made. One of the first factories was that at Saint-Cloud near Paris, established in 1693. However, it was not until 1710 that the first factory to make true 'hard-paste' porcelain was established at Meissen in Germany [7]. During the 18th century, porcelain manufacture spread throughout Europe, and state support enabled some factories to reach standards which can never be equalled. Glasgow's collection of continental porcelain is neither large nor rich, but it does contain pieces from the principal factories of Meissen and Sèvres as well as from lesser factories and there is an emphasis on French porcelain, particularly the wares of Saint-Cloud and Chantilly.

4. *Tin-glazed bowl from Talavera de la Reyna, Spanish, late 17th century, diameter 47cm (18⅛in).*

5. *Flower brick, tin-glazed earthenware, made by Albertus Kiehl at the White Star Pottery, The Hague, between 1761 and 1772, length 26cm (10¼in).*

6. *Group of German stonewares, left to right: Sieburg 'Schnelle' tankard; Raren jar; Kreussen tankard; Cologne 'Bellarmine' bottle, all c.1580-1650; height of Schnelle 38.5cm (15¼in).*

7. *Porcelain tea and coffee service, Meissen, 1720s, diameter of saucers 12cm (4¾in).*

British Ceramics

Glasgow's collection of ceramics inevitably favours British wares and reflects their development from the 17th century [8] to the present day. The rise of the Staffordshire potteries is chronicled by means of a small but interesting group from early wares to modern industrial pieces. Many of the significant products developed in the 18th century are represented, 'agate wares' of coloured clays, variegated wares with mottled glazes, salt-glazed stonewares and so forth. Finer Wedgwood wares, including the familiar green or blue Jasper ware and black Basaltes, dramatically demonstrate the rapid developments in the Staffordshire industry at the period. About ninety pieces of cream coloured earthenware (creamware) from Wedgwood and other British makers represent this significant product. Creamware was extremely successful, widely made and exported in huge quantities to many overseas markets.

Although there was no state patronage of factories to equal that on the Continent, porcelain was made in England from the middle of the 18th century. Generally, 'soft-paste' porcelains were produced. Pieces from several of the English factories are housed at Kelvingrove, amongst them Chelsea and Bow in London, and Derby. The principal group, however, is of ware from Worcester [9], and from Caughley, which was sited slightly farther up the River Severn. This group comprises some four hundred items, many of them decorated not with freehand painting but with prints transferred from engraved copper plates, one of the technical advances of the period over the traditional hand method. Porcelain and bone china, a type of artificial porcelain, from Rockingham, Spode, Coalport, Minton and other leading factories brings the collection into the 19th century.

The range of ceramics produced in Victorian Britain was vast, and few collections can hope to do it justice. That in Glasgow reflects many of the important and characteristic wares. The largest group comprises transfer-printed earthenwares, both English and Scottish.

10. Parian figure of Miranda by John Bell, made by Minton, c.1850, height 37cm (14¼in).

8. Staffordshire slipware mug formerly in the Solon collection, late 17th century, height 10cm (4in).

9. Worcester porcelain mugs decorated with transfer prints of 'The Harvesters' and 'The Minuet', both engraved by Robert Hancock, English, c.1760, height 8.4cm (3¼in).

Humble Staffordshire chimney ornaments contrast with opulent wares from more renowned factories. Everything from utilitarian salt-glazed stonewares to fine Parian (an imitation of white marble) [10] has a place in the collection. Within the general scope of this section there are particular strengths. A number of commemorative wares, for example, celebrate the Royal Jubilees of 1887 and 1897, as well as other personalities and events.

There is also a large group of lustrewares [11] based upon a private collection gifted in 1938, which principally concentrates on Staffordshire products of the early 19th century. These wares have a lustrous finish derived from copper, platinum or other metals incorporated in the glaze.

Scottish Pottery

Although much work has been done recently, the field of Scottish pottery is still comparatively unstudied. The only comprehensive book on the subject was published by J. Arnold Fleming as long ago as 1923, and Glasgow is fortunate in having part of the author's collection which contained some magnificent items. The range of Scottish pottery is far wider than many suppose, and reflects the whole spectrum of British ceramics. The collection at Kelvingrove has pieces originating from all over Scotland, but with an emphasis upon West coast potteries in general and those of the Glasgow area in particular. In scope it ranges from the crude earthenwares of local country potteries to fine porcelains. Most of the pieces date from the 19th century, when Glasgow and its pottery industry were expanding rapidly. Some items, however, are earlier, and there is, for example, a growing number of pieces attributed to the Delftfield Pottery [12]. This interesting Glasgow company was set up in 1748 to make tin-glazed earthenwares and was the only Scottish pottery to produce them. The company eventually made white stonewares, creamware, pearlware and other bodies, and was finally dissolved in 1823.

11. *Lustreware jug by Dixon & Co., Sunderland, early 19th century, height 13.5cm (5¼in).*

12. *Tin-glazed earthenware bottle attributed to the Delftfield Pottery, Glasgow, c.1760, height 24cm (9½in).*

Potteries in Scotland made almost every conceivable type of ceramic product. Ordinary domestic utensils and tablewares, brightly coloured cottage ornaments, enamalled porcelain tea services, printed jugs and punchbowls, stoneware jars, bottles and containers, sanitaryware and carpet bowls indicate the breadth of production [14]. Domestic wares of all standards were manufactured, and like the humbler sponge-decorated wares, many of these were designed specifically for the growing export markets. Everything from fine porcelains [13] to drainpipes came from Glasgow, including slip-decorated red earthenwares with incised mottoes from Cumnock and agate wares of marbled clays from Aberdeen. Transfer-printed earthenwares were made throughout the Scottish industry. Some of the wares followed English prototypes, but most had a distinctive Scottish character. Potteries ranged from tiny country sites to huge urban plants using industrial techniques of mass production.

13. *Bone china teacup and saucer from J. & M.P. Bell's Pottery, Glasgow, 19th century; diameter of saucer 14cm (5½in).*

14. *Group of 19th-century Scottish wares.*

15. *Ceramic sculpture made in 1975 by David Cohen, an American potter resident in Scotland, height 42cm (16¼in).*

16. *Stoneware jug modelled and decorated by Frank A. Butler, Mary Thomson and Emily A. London, bought directly from Doulton & Co. in 1878 for 30 shillings (£1.50), height 20.5cm (8in).*

17. *Work by some of the pioneer studio potters, left to right: vases by William Staite Murray, Nora Braden, Katherine Pleydell Bouverie, Bernard Leach; bowl by Michael Cardew; diameter of bowl 32cm (12¼in).*

Studio/Art Pottery

The Arts and Crafts movement arose as a reaction to the growing industrial domination of late-19th-century Britain. One aspect of it was a growing interest in 'Art' pottery, which was carefully designed and often made in small workshops rather than factories. Glasgow is well endowed with pieces from most of the leading potteries of the day, some of which were bought directly from the makers. Chief amongst these is a fine group of wares from Doulton & Co. [16] and James Stiff & Co., adjacent factories in Lambeth in London. Wares from Sir Edmund Elton's Sunflower Pottery at Clevedon in Somerset, William de Morgan (who worked in London), Bretby in Woodville, Derbyshire, and from the Ruskin Pottery at Smethwick are included in the collection, and there is a good selection from the Della Robbia Pottery in Birkenhead. Scottish Art wares are represented by a large collection of pieces from the Dunmore Pottery, Falkirk.

Around the turn of the century a new attitude to pottery began to develop, and individual artist craftsmen came into their own. The work of the Martin Brothers in Lambeth and Southall is well known, but that of Hugh Allan at Milngavie near Glasgow is not. His Allander Pottery was worked only between 1904 and 1908 and was not very productive. Glasgow has a good number of these rare pieces, some of which were bought from the maker's sister in 1914. After the First World War a new younger generation of potters began to show a more intense approach, which transformed their craft into an art. Because they generally used small private workshops, they are known as 'studio potters'. In 1943 and 1944 the Contemporary Arts Society presented to the city wares by Bernard Leach, William Staite Murray, Katherine Pleydell Bouverie, Nora Braden and Michael Cardew. This fine group of pots formed the basis of the studio pottery collection [17] which was developed in the 1960s with several purchases, principally from Scottish potters. When the Decorative Arts Department was formed in 1974 a whole series of purchases was made from artists of the calibre of Jacqueline Poncelet, Alan Caiger Smith, Michael Casson and Richard Batterham. Subsequently the collection has been extended, and today aims to represent contemporary Scottish ceramics [15], whilst reflecting developments in British Studio pottery as a whole.

The Seton Murray Thomson Collection

The horse has for centuries been one of man's closest associates in the animal kingdom, in peace and war his major source of power. It is perhaps surprising, therefore, that few thematic collectors seem to have selected the horse as their subject. The Seton Murray Thomson collection is the only one of such size and variety in any British museum.

Thomson's sole criterion for an object for his collection was whether it was a good representation of a horse. The 449 items range from Tang horses to celluloid toys, from an ancient Cypriote earthenware to modern European porcelain. They come from nineteen different countries and are made of over thirty materials including jade, chalcedony, rock crystal, malachite, soapstone, ivory, amber, wood, iron, bronze, brass, silver, porcelain, papier-mâché [1], pottery [2], celluloid, mother-of-pearl, bone, rubber, glass, wax and alabaster.

The collection was assembled between 1923 and 1933 from an enormous variety of sources: from the sales of great collections, from the auction houses of London and the provinces, from antique shops and toyshops, from the Burlington Arcade and from Woolworth. An example of the collector's patience and selectivity was his search for a fine set of the eight horses of Mu Wang — a group of horses in varying

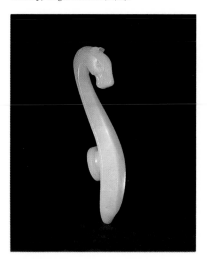

2. Pair of tin-glazed Hispano-Moresque earthenware candleholders, Spanish, 17th century, height 24.8cm (9¾in).

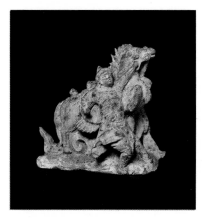

3. Jade buckle, Chinese, date unknown, length 12.7cm (5in).

4. Glazed earthenware horse with man on each side, Chinese, Tang Dynasty 618-907 A.D., height 15.9cm (6¼in).

1. Papier-mâché horse covered with hair, Japanese, 18th or 19th century, height 30.5cm (12in).

postures representing those which drew the chariot of the Emperor Mu Wang (Chang dynasty) on a journey to the Western Gardens in search of the Peach of Immortality. Eventually five examples were acquired, but at least one set was lost to the collection because by the time the reply to the Peking dealer's offer, sent by the quickest route, via Siberia, arrived, it had been sold.

The collection divides into four main geographical groups. The largest in number come from China and take many forms, from ridge tiles to jade buckles [3], illustrating the skill of the Oriental craftsmen in a variety of ceramic materials [4] as well as a wide range of hard and soft natural materials. The next largest group are English in origin, mainly ceramics of the 19th century. These range from the elegant Leeds stallion [8] through the more popular 'fairings' — objects sold at fairs — to a Worcester porcelain lady on a bay hunter, modelled by Doris Lindman. A tiny but interesting group consists of three wax models of horse and jockey produced to commemorate the Derby winners of 1817 and 1818 — 'Azob' and 'Sam'.

The European group covers a wider range of materials and date than the English. The most outstanding pieces here are a 17th-century wooden horse with glass eyes, complete with harness and saddle in blue velvet edged with silver braid; a water-gilt bronze [7] by Antonio Susini (died 1624) after a model by Giambologna; and a late 19th-century Austrian meerschaum pipe.

The smallest group consists of items from early Mediterranean [6] and African [5] cultures and includes a Cypriote horse dating from the 15th century B.C. — the oldest in the collection.

5. *Carved wooden striped horse or zebra, Barotse tribe, East Africa, height 15.2cm (6in).*

6. *Horse and rider in clay, Greek, 6th century B.C., height 11.4cm (4¼in).*

7. *Water-gilt bronze horse on marble base, by Antonio Susini, a craftsman in the workshop of Giovanni da Bologna, Italian, 17th century, height 31.8cm (12½in).*

8. *Enamelled earthenware stallion, English, 19th century, height 43.2cm (17in).*

Fine Art

Introduction

The Fine Art Collection at Kelvingrove consists of over 3,000 oil paintings, 12,500 prints and drawings and 300 pieces of sculpture. Most schools and periods are represented but the greatest strengths lie in Dutch 17th and French 19th-century painting and in Scottish art in all media from the 18th century to the present day.

The founder of the collection was Archibald McLellan (1797-1854) [1], a wealthy Glasgow coach-builder and a man of wide cultural and civic interests. He bequeathed to his native city several hundred oil paintings mainly by Italian, Dutch and Flemish artists, as well as some British pictures and pieces of sculpture. Unfortunately, he died insolvent, and the then Glasgow Corporation had to be persuaded to buy the collection along with the galleries in which it was housed [2]. These, as The McLellan Galleries, although no longer a part of the museum complex, still exist in Sauchiehall Street in Glasgow. The strongest aspect of McLellan's collection was Italian art of the 16th and 17th centuries, and to this day the great majority of the works displayed in the Italian gallery at Kelvingrove derive from his bequest. Most notable of all his paintings is *The adulteress brought before Christ* which is attributed to Giorgione (see page 104).

Other gifts and bequests soon followed McLellan's and indeed the collection relied almost entirely on these sources until the 1890s when more frequent purchasing began. Most of the early benefactors

1. *Robert Cree Crawford (1842-1924)* after *John Graham-Gilbert (1794-1866)* Archibald McLellan *(1797-1854), detail, 1839, canvas 247.6 × 165.1cm (97½ × 65in).*

2. *Interior of the McLellan Galleries in the 1890s.*

3. *William Brodie (1815-1881)* John Graham-Gilbert *(1794-1866) detail, 1870, marble, height 190cm (74⅞in).*

were local people who had made fortunes in Glasgow's rapidly expanding industries, but although their business careers are well documented, regrettably little is known about their collecting habits as in only a few cases have detailed purchase records come to light.

In the 1870s the generosity of two men almost completed the old-master Dutch and Flemish collection as it stands today. In 1874 came the bequest of over 100 pictures from William Euing (1788-1874), a leading Glasgow figure in marine insurance, and three years later the widow of the portrait painter John Graham-Gilbert (1794-1866) [3] bequeathed his collection of 70 paintings, which included Rembrandt's *Man in armour* (see page 123).

In 1892 James Orrock presented what is still the gallery's finest group of English watercolours, and four years later a small but highly significant selection of British, Dutch and French oil paintings was given to the gallery by the family of the late James Reid of Auchterarder (1823-1894) [4], who had been Director of Neilson, Reid's Hyde-park Locomotive Works in Glasgow, the biggest concern of its kind in Europe. The Reid Gift included the gallery's only oils by Constable and Turner as well as works by Corot, Troyon and Jacque which formed the nucleus of the now famous 19th-century French collection.

4. *Sir George Reid (1841-1913)* James Reid of Auchterarder *(1823-1894), detail, canvas 144.8 × 97.8cm (57 × 38½in).*

Also of outstanding importance during this period was one of the gallery's first purchases. In 1891, under pressure from a group of local artists, led by James Guthrie and other Glasgow Boys, the Corporation bought Whistler's *Arrangement in grey and black no. 2: Portrait of Thomas Carlyle* (see page 155). Other purchases soon followed — including oils, watercolours and sculpture by the Glasgow Boys — but the collection relied mainly on gifts and bequests until well into the 20th century.

In 1900 came the gift, from his family, of the first of a number of pictures which eventually came to the gallery from the collection of the late Dr James 'Paraffin' Young (1811-1883), the Glasgow-born pioneer of the Scottish oil industry. His treasures included the two huge landscapes by Salvator Rosa which had been acquired in 1877 by his agents in Florence from descendants of the family which had originally commissioned them.

Perhaps the most important early 20th-century bequest was that of James Donald (1830-1905), a local chemical manufacturer, whose collection consisted almost entirely of 19th-century Dutch, French and British oil paintings and watercolours. His French Barbizon and Realist pictures gave the gallery a good foundation on which the Impressionist collection was later built. Notable British oils acquired around this time included Raeburn portraits from the Isabella Campbell Bequest and works by Burne-Jones and Albert Moore which had originally been commissioned by William Connal, a Glasgow pig-iron manufacturer.

Interest in French paintings by James Donald and later collectors was promoted locally after 1874, when Craibe Angus, the first Scottish dealer to specialize in Hague and Barbizon School pictures, opened a commercial gallery in Glasgow. Among the many other dealers who commenced business in the city around this time was the highly influential Alexander Reid (1854-1928) [5] who was selling Impressionist pictures in Glasgow as early as 1890. Reid's taste is

5. *Vincent van Gogh (1853-1890)* Portrait of Alexander Reid (1854-1928), *board 42 × 33cm (16¼ × 13in).*

6. *Leslie Hunter (1877-1931)* Portrait of William McInnes (1868-1944), *canvas 45.7 × 38.1cm (18 × 15in).*

reflected in Kelvingrove's French collection as many of its benefactors were his customers.

From the 1920s onwards the gallery began to collect prints. Drawings and watercolours had been acquired since the earliest days, but print collecting was not taken seriously until 1920 when John Innes presented over 250 old-master and 19th-century items. Important purchases for the new Print Room were soon made, among them groups of works by Piranesi and Rossini, Daumier and Gauguin, while subsequent additions have tended to concentrate on the British, especially the Scottish, school.

In 1927 a unique and most generous benefactor, The Hamilton Trust, came into existence. This fund of money derived from the estates of members of a Glasgow family, John, Elizabeth and Christina Hamilton, who stipulated that it was to be used for the purchase of a collection of oil paintings for Kelvingrove. The Trust, which is still in operation, has presented over 70 pictures, nearly all of British or French origin and including works by Monet, Gauguin, Signac, Ramsay, Rossetti and Eardley.

The most important individual 20th-century benefactor to date has been William McInnes (1868-1944) [6], a Glasgow shipowner who left to his native city his entire collection of over 70 paintings as well as prints, drawings, silver, ceramics and glass. The bequest included 33 French works (many of them bought from Alexander Reid) by key artists such as Monet, Degas, Renoir, van Gogh, Cézanne and Picasso, while the British pictures were mostly by the Glasgow Boys and the Scottish Colourists, of whom he was a regular patron. This donation firmly established the international importance of Glasgow's French collection.

Since the Second World War major gifts and bequests have become increasingly scarce, and in recent years the gallery has concentrated on purchasing items mainly to fill gaps in the French collection [7] and to expand the holdings of British paintings, prints, drawings and sculpture. Old-master purchases have of necessity been few but notable among them was *Head of a man,* the fragment from Giorgione's *Adulteress,* which was bought at auction in 1971 (see page 104). French pictures purchased have included van Gogh's *Portrait of Alexander Reid* as well as works by Luce, Breton and Bernard.

7. *The French gallery, 1985.*

Very many of the Gallery's British paintings [8] have been acquired by purchase because, surprisingly, there were no donations to that school of the significance which, say, the McLellan, Graham-Gilbert or Donald Bequests had to the Continental schools. Instead, British paintings came from a wider variety of collectors, while the greater quantity of purchases reflects not only the availability of such work but also — until recently — its much lower price range. The collection of pre-19th-century Scottish oil paintings has been greatly enlarged by postwar additions including works by Aikman, Jacob More, Gavin Hamilton and David Allan. Most contemporary works, in all media, are purchases, and the Gallery aims to acquire items by local artists who have attained wider significance. Patronage having moved from the private to the public sector, financial assistance for most purchases is now sought from various cultural and governmental organizations.

8. *British gallery I, 1985.*

Italian Painting

The history of Italian art encompasses such a great variety of styles and talents that very few collections are able fully to portray its development. It is remarkable, therefore, that although the Italian collection at Kelvingrove is modest in size, it nonetheless illustrates most of the main currents in Italian art. If the periods before 1450 and after 1800 are thinly represented, this is amply compensated for by the thorough coverage of Renaissance and Baroque art, often in paintings by some of the most renowned artists of their times.

The earliest Italian painting in the collection was probably once part of a large, multi-panelled altarpiece. It shows St Lawrence [1] holding a palm and a gridiron, the symbols of his martyrdom. The rich gold-leaf background, into which intricate patterns have been incised, is typical of Sienese painting in the 14th century. The panel is attributed to one of the most refined artists of that school, Paolo di Giovanni Fei (*c.*1345-1411), and is a good example of the Byzantine-influenced manner of painting practised by many 14th-century artists. This style gave way to a much more natural one in the new era of the Renaissance (the term means 'rebirth' or 'revival'), which lasted from about 1400 to 1520.

In the 15th century, while other countries were growing into strong kingdoms, Italy still consisted of city-states vying with each other in commerce, war and the arts. One result of this rivalry was the emergence in the main cities of separate schools of painting. If these differed in particulars such as the use of line and colour, in general they all adhered to the Renaissance ideal of truth to nature, achieved by a combination of observation, science, and a study of ancient Greek and Roman art. This new illusion of reality made the viewer feel as if he too was experiencing the events portrayed by the painted figures, a sense admirably conveyed by Francesco Francia (*c.*1450-1517/18) in *The Nativity* [3]. Here the figures seem to breathe and to move in space: they have weight and volume; there is a uniform light; and objects are made to recede convincingly into the distance by means of the newly discovered science of perspective.

The idea of making art a mirror of reality was developed even fur-

1. *Paolo di Giovanni Fei (c.1345-1411)* St Lawrence, *tempera on wood 63.5 × 30.5cm (25 × 12in).*

2. *Giovanni Bellini (active c.1459-died 1516)* The Madonna with the Child blessing, *c.1475, wood 62.2 × 46.4cm (24¼ × 18¼in).*

3. *Francesco Francia (1450?-1517)* The Nativity, *c.1494, wood 28.9 × 54.9 cm (11¾ × 21⅝in).*

4. *Vincenzo Catena (active c.1500-1531)* The Madonna and Child with Saints Catherine and Mary Magdalene, *c.1507, wood 61.6 × 83.5cm (24¼ × 32⅞in).*

ther by Giovanni Bellini (active *c.*1459-died 1516), whose main contribution to the Renaissance lay in his amazing sensitivity to colour. He is represented in the collection by *The Madonna with the Child blessing* [2]. The great German artist Albrecht Dürer met Bellini in Venice in 1506 and wrote of him in one of his letters: 'He is very old, but still the best in painting.' Bellini was certainly the greatest Venetian artist of the 15th century, and his workshop included many painters who were to rise to prominence after 1500. They too employed the brightest of hues in their pictures.

5. *Filippino Lippi (1457?-1504)* The Madonna and Child with the infant St John and two angels, *mid 1480s, tempera on wood, diameter 118.4cm (46⅝in).*

6. *Sandro Botticelli (c.1445-1510)* The Annunciation, *late 1490s, tempera on wood, 49.5 × 61.9cm (19½ × 24¾in).*

The Venetian artists' use of rich colour is particularly apparent if one compares pictures of the Virgin and Child by Vincenzo Catena (active *c.*1500-1531) [4], who was a follower of Bellini, and Filippino Lippi (1457?-1504) [5], who was based in Florence. Although each artist arrives at a similarly symmetrical composition, Lippi's colours are much more restrained, partly because of his use of tempera rather than oil and because he depends to a greater extent on line as a means of emotional expression. He also takes greater liberties with the proportions of the figures, in order to make them seem more elegant and refined. This kind of painting has been termed Quattrocento Mannerism (from the Italian for 15th century), because it permits the bending of rules and anticipates the more widespread style of that

name in the following century. Sandro Botticelli (*c.*1445-1510), Lippi's master, was in fact the main exponent of the style, as well as being the most individual painter in Florence at the end of the 15th century. In his painting of *The Annunciation* [6] the central piers of the building are inclined from the vertical, thus accentuating the drama of the event.

Just as the culture, sophistication and refinement of Lorenzo de' Medici's court in Florence found expression in Botticelli's art, so too the cultural life of Venice influenced Giorgione (1478?-1510). He was born in Castelfranco, 30 miles northwest of the city, and in the opinion of a contemporary, Giorgio Vasari, he followed in the footsteps of Leonardo da Vinci. Today Giorgione is appreciated as one of the first artists to create a predominantly emotional atmosphere in his works. These contain an air of mystery, and it is perhaps this quality above all which supports the attribution of *The adultress brought before Christ* [7] to him. The early ownership of the painting, too, is obscure but later, in the 17th century, it belonged to Queen Christina of Sweden. At some stage the figure at the far right of the composition was cut away, although fortunately not all of it was lost. In 1971 the Gallery acquired the painting of the head [8] at auction.

7. Attributed to Giorgio da Castelfranco, called Giorgione (1478?-1510) The adulteress brought before Christ, c.1508-1510, canvas 139.2 × 181.7cm (54⅞ × 71¼in).

8. Attributed to Giorgio da Castelfranco, called Giorgione (1478?-1510) Head of a man, c.1508-1510, canvas 47 × 40.5cm (18½ × 16in).

9. *Paris Bordone (1500-1571)* The Madonna
and Child with Saints John the Baptist,
Mary Magdalene and Liberale, c.*1525, wood*
85.4 × 117.5cm (33¾ × 46¼in).

10. *Girolamo da Carpi (1501-1556)* The Holy
Family with St Catherine and the infant
St John, *early 1550s, wood 61.5 × 82cm*
(24¼ × 32¼in).

11. *Giuseppe Cesari,* called *Cavaliere d'Arpino*
(1568-1640) The Archangel Michael and the
rebel angels, c.*1593, copper 57.8 × 41.8cm*
(22¾ × 16¼in).

Despite Giorgione's tragic early death from the plague in 1510, he
was to have many followers in Venice. These included Vincenzo Catena and Titian, the latter becoming in his turn the most influential
Venetian painter. He developed to new heights the so-called *sacra
conversazione* subject, in which the Madonna and Child were usually
placed in a landscape setting and accompanied by saints and sometimes also by likenesses of the donors who commissioned the paintings. Paris Bordone (1500-1571), who was in Venice by 1518, was
influenced by Titian in his own handling of such subjects [9], but the
less relaxed poses of his figures contain a hint of the Mannerist style
(as distinct from Quattrocento Mannerism) which then prevailed
elsewhere in Italy and which signalled the end of the Renaissance.

Girolamo da Carpi (1501-1556), in his *The Holy Family with St Catherine and the infant St John* [10], departs from Renaissance clarity of meaning when he combines several subjects in one scene: the meeting of Christ and St John the Baptist as infants, the mystical marriage of St Catherine, and the rest of the Holy Family during the flight into Egypt. Such visual and intellectual complexity is a typical feature of Mannerism, as is a concentration on the nude, usually represented in elaborate poses and energetic motion. The latter characteristic is strikingly apparent in *The Archangel Michael and the rebel angels* by Cavaliere d'Arpino (1568-1640) [11], who was a leading late Mannerist in Rome. In this painting, St Michael expels from Heaven the angels who refused to fight the Devil in their midst. It is perhaps no accident that the artist has depicted that moment in the story when the forces of Heaven are victorious, for the prevailing spirit in Rome at that time was one of the 'Church Triumphant'. After the doubts resulting from the Reformation and the Sack of Rome, the Counter-Reformation strove to reassert Catholic dogma, eventually leading to a new period of intense religiosity, self-confidence and dynamism. These qualities were reflected in the art of the time (*c.*1590-*c.*1710), which is known as the Baroque. In contrast to Mannerism, it was an art designed primarily to appeal to the masses by a greater clarity of style and simplicity of presentation.

Although the cities of 17th-century Italy continued to support their own schools of painting, the stylistic differences between them were no longer so obvious. Artists moved freely from place to place, and their links with fellow painters were less dictated by geographical and personal ties. Caravaggio (1571/2-1610) and Annibale Carracci (1560-1609) were the two most influential Italian painters of their day, and although neither is represented in the collection, there are notable works by some of their followers.

12. *Antiveduto Gramatica (c. 1570-1626)* The Madonna and Child with St Anne, *canvas 95.4 × 133cm (37⅝ × 52⅜in).*

13. *Jusepe de Ribera*, called *Lo Spagnoletto* *(1591-1652)* St Peter repentant, *1628, canvas* *124 × 97.8cm (48¾ × 38½in).*

14. *Domenico Zampieri*, called *Domenichino* *(1581-1641)* St Jerome in a landscape, *c.1610, wood 44 × 59.8cm (17⅜ × 23½in).*

15. *Salvator Rosa (1615-1673)* St John the Baptist in the wilderness, *1650s, canvas* *173.4 × 260.7cm (68¼ × 102⅝in).*

Caravaggio worked in the studio of Antiveduto Gramatica (*c.*1570-1626) in Rome in 1594, whilst the Spaniard, Jusepe de Ribera (1591-1652), who settled in Naples in 1616, was one of the most prominent and influential of the so-called *Caravaggisti.* Gramatica's *The Madonna and Child with St Anne* [12] is indebted to Caravaggio in its use of strong contrasts of light and shade and realistically conceived figures, making for an immediacy new in Italian art. The same features appear in Ribera's *St Peter repentant* [13], a popular 17th-century subject which reminded people that although he was a saint, Peter had still been an ordinary man prone to human error.

16. *Giovanni Battista Salvi*, called *Sassoferrato (1609-1685)* The Madonna and Child with St Elisabeth and the infant St John, *canvas 73.3 × 98.4 cm (28⅞ × 38¾in).*

Annibale Carracci was an adherent of a classical type of painting based on harmonious design and idealized forms, as distinct from Caravaggio whose art was almost brutally real. Like Caravaggio he attracted many followers, notably Domenichino (1581-1641), whose *St Jerome in a landscape* [14] derives a number of its features from Carracci's art. Unlike his master, however, the younger artist uses landscape as an integral part of the picture, thus paving the way for painters such as Salvator Rosa (1615-1673) who endowed the genre of landscape with a credibility which it had hitherto lacked in Italy. *St John the Baptist in the wilderness* [15] is an example of the wild, 'savage' type of landscape which established Rosa's tremendous popularity in 18th-century Britain, and which epitomized for the British the essential qualities of 'the sublime'.

Many 17th-century Italian artists cannot be neatly associated with any general artistic trend. Sassoferrato (1609-1685), in *The Madonna and Child with St Elisabeth and the infant St John* [16], turns to the Renaissance and the classicism of Annibale Carracci for inspiration. The calm serenity of his figures is thus at variance with the rhetorical gesturing and dramatic lighting generally associated with the Baroque. In the same way, *Salome with the head of John the Baptist* [17] by the Florentine Carlo Dolci (1616-1686) contrasts with the usually more violent treatment of the subject by his contemporaries. He plays down the horror of the event, instead making his image as realistic as possible with a painstakingly meticulous technique.

In the 18th century, Italian landscape painting gained new impetus, partly because lessening Papal influence on the arts resulted in the acceptance of a wider range of subject matter, but also because the many travellers to Italy at that time wanted souvenirs of their journeys. In *View of Ariccia* [18] by Paolo Anesi (active 1723-1766), the artist has adeptly combined a charming landscape with a topographically accurate view of a town near Rome. The scene is dominated

17. *Carlo Dolci (1616-1686)* Salome with the head of John the Baptist, c.*1680, canvas 123.1 × 95.2cm (48½ × 37¼in).*

by the church of Santa Maria dell'Assunzione, built by the Baroque architect Gianlorenzo Bernini between 1662 and 1664. Similarly, Francesco Guardi (1712-1793) has made a famous building, the church designed by Andrea Palladio in 1565, the centrepiece of his *View of the Church of San Giorgio Maggiore, Venice* [19]. Guardi was also attracted by the atmospheric lighting and the picturesque boats, all of which he renders with a free handling of paint. Together with Canaletto (1697-1768), who greatly influenced him, Guardi has always been immensely popular with British collectors.

18. *Paolo Anesi (active 1723-1766)* View of Ariccia, *canvas 59 × 85.1cm (23¼ × 33½in).*

19. *Francesco Guardi (1712-1793)* View of the Church of San Giorgio Maggiore, Venice, *c.1755, canvas 71.1 × 119.7cm (28 × 47¼in).*

20. *Francesco Zuccarelli (1702-1788)* St John the Baptist preaching, c.*1750s, canvas 67.1 × 51.4cm (26¼ × 20¼in).*

Francesco Zuccarelli (1702-1788) had an enormous reputation as a landscapist, particularly in England where he was a founder member of the Royal Academy in 1768. Like Salvator Rosa before him, in his painting of a scene from the life of St John the Baptist, he subordinates the biblical event to a fanciful landscape [20]. Zuccarelli, however, lacks the high-pitched drama of Rosa, and is primarily concerned to produce a pleasing decorative effect. The difference is symptomatic of the change in outlook between the art of the 17th and 18th centuries.

By the time of Guardi's death in 1793, the great age of Italian painting had ended. But the enormous influence it has exerted on artists continues up to the present day, and is markedly evident in *Christ of St John of the Cross* [21] which was painted by Salvador Dali (born 1904) in 1951. This Spaniard was a pioneer of the Surrealist movement in painting, but his later religious works have also attracted much attention. Dali's vision of Christ crucified is highly novel, for the cross is suspended in space and dramatically foreshortened, whilst the finely polished technique is totally unlike most contemporary methods of painting. These devices heighten the impact of the picture, which is one of the most important examples of 20th-century religious art.

21. *Salvador Dali (born 1904)* Christ of St John of the Cross, *1951, canvas 204.8 × 115.9cm (80¾ × 45⅝in).*

Dutch, Flemish and German Painting

The great periods of Flemish and Dutch art were the 15th and 17th centuries respectively. Although the earlier period is not represented in the collection, Glasgow has strong holdings of later Flemish art and of Dutch paintings from the Golden Age. The collection of the latter is large enough to display both great variety and a degree of specialization, for some of the major figures are represented by several works. The collection also contains a number of paintings by the 19th-century Hague School of artists.

The three modern nations of the Netherlands, Belgium and Luxembourg did not exist as such until the end of the 16th century, for the whole area was under Spanish rule and as yet no political boundaries divided north from south. The south was, however, richer, and the cities of Bruges, Ghent, Antwerp and Brussels were great centres both of commerce and the arts.

Bernard van Orley (c.1488-1541) worked in Brussels as court painter to two successive Spanish Regents — a position which probably saved him from punishment when he was arrested by the Inquisition in 1527 for listening to Protestant sermons. Despite this, his painting of *The Virgin and Child by a fountain* [1] adheres very closely to the liturgical requirements of the Catholic Church; the Virgin's humility and virginity, for instance, are signified by the fact that she is seated on the ground in 'a garden enclosed'. At the same time, the rich colouring and exquisite detail of the picture give a feeling of reality.

An interest in describing human beings and their environment as faithfully as possible is one of the dominant characteristics of northern European painting between the 15th and 17th centuries. When he painted *The conversion of St Eustace* [2], the German artist

1. *Bernard van Orley (c.1488-1541)* The Virgin and Child by a fountain, *wood 105.4 × 82.2cm (41¼ × 32⅜in).*

2. *Hans Mielich (1516-1573)* The conversion of St Eustace, *c.1538, wood 55.9 × 41.3cm (22 × 16¼in).*

3. *Attributed to Jan Bruegel the Younger (1601-1679)* An allegorical landscape — autumn, *wood 73.6 × 114.6cm (29 × 45¼in).*

4. *Peter Paul Rubens (1577-1640) and Jan Bruegel the Elder (1568-1628)* Nature adorned by the Graces, *c.1615, wood 106.7 × 72.4cm (42 × 28½in).*

5. Jacob Jordaens (1593-1678) The fruit seller, c.1635-1640, canvas 119.6 × 157.1cm (47¼ × 61⅝in).

Hans Mielich (1516-1573) depicted familiar costumes and scenery with surprising truthfulness. As a result, the picture tells modern viewers as much about life in the 16th century as it does about the legend of the saint, who was a Roman general converted to Christianity by the miraculous appearance of a stag with a crucifix between its antlers.

The gradual secularization of Flemish art is reflected in works by Peter Paul Rubens, Jacob Jordaens, Jan Bruegel the Younger and David Teniers the Younger. After his return from Italy to Antwerp in 1608, Rubens (1577-1640) rapidly developed into one of the foremost artists of the period. He became court painter to the Spanish Governors of the Netherlands, and in later life was also in demand at the courts of England and France. His prodigious output included large-scale historical and religious paintings as well as more informal and light-hearted works. *Nature adorned by the Graces* [4] falls into the second category and is generally concerned with the idea of Nature and her fruitfulness: a garland is being hauled into position to form a decorative bower surrounding the statue of Mother Nature. The figures were painted by Rubens, but he employed his friend and assistant, Jan Bruegel the Elder (1568-1628), to execute the garland and numerous small animals in a highly detailed style. A successful painter in his own right, Bruegel ran a large workshop in which his son, Jan Bruegel the Younger (1601-1679), was an apprentice. The latter's pictures of the seasons likewise celebrate Nature's bounty[3].

Jacob Jordaens (1593-1678) started his career as an assistant in the atelier of Rubens, and eventually succeeded him as the leading painter in Antwerp. Although he never travelled to Italy, like most of his contemporaries he was greatly influenced by Italian artists, especially Caravaggio, whose dramatic light effects and realistic figure types are echoed in *The fruit seller* [5]. At the time it was unusual for an artist to base such a large painting on an everyday subject, and it is a measure of Jordaens' genius that he was able to endow the humble scene with dignity and lasting significance. David Teniers the

6. David Teniers the Younger (1610-1690) A surgeon treating a peasant's foot, *wood* 36.8 × 27.3cm (14½ × 10¾in).

7. *Attributed to Nicolaes Eliasz, called
Pickenoy (1590/1-1654/6)* Portrait of a
fifteen year old girl, *1633, wood 71.7 × 54.3cm
(28¼ × 21⅜in).*

8. *Bartholomeus van der Helst (1613-1670)*
Portrait of a naval commander, *1662, canvas
113 × 91.4cm (44½ × 36in).*

9. *Frans van Mieris the Elder (1635-1681)*
A sick woman and her doctor, *1657, copper
34.3 × 27.3cm (13½ × 10¾in).*

Younger (1610-1690), who specialized in small genre scenes, probably had a similar end in mind when he painted *A surgeon treating a peasant's foot* [6], in which objects, figures and interior are unified by a skilful disposition of light.

The predominantly Protestant northern provinces of The Netherlands gained independence from Spain in 1579 when they formed a Dutch republic. By about 1600, after a complex series of revolts, the evolution of the republic was virtually complete, and it could concentrate on economic rather than military affairs. Over the next few decades it rapidly developed into one of the great commercial powers of Europe and the centre of an overseas empire. This growth was accompanied by a tremendous outburst of artistic activity, with cities such as Amsterdam, Haarlem, Leiden and Delft being rich enough to support large numbers of painters. Competition was fierce, and most artists concentrated on one type of subject which they would perfect to a very high standard. Because of this, it is usual to discuss 17th-century Dutch art in terms of subject categories.

Nicolaes Eliasz (1590/1-1654/6) was one of the most successful portrait painters in Amsterdam. His ability to capture a good likeness and render the textures of cloth and skin made him very popular among the middle classes [7]. These qualities are also found in the portraits of Eliasz's pupil, Bartholomeus van der Helst (1613-1670), who was the most famous portraitist in Amsterdam in the 1650s. His approach tended to be a little more formal, as can be seen in *Portrait of a naval commander* [8] which may represent Captain Willem van der Zaan (1621-1669). He wears the type of medal and chain awarded to commanders who captured one or more enemy ships.

10. *Willem Kalf (1619-1693)* Still life, *canvas*
83.8 × 69.8cm (33 × 27¼in).

Whereas portraiture frequently has as subjects individuals who are important, genre painting often provides an insight into the customs, habits, behaviour and appearance of ordinary people. Certain subjects, such as that of the lovesick woman, were so popular that they entered the standard vocabulary of art, and if anything is radical or new in the version painted by Frans van Mieris the Elder (1635-1681) it is the remarkably high degree of finish [9]. Van Mieris was the leading member of the Leiden school of *fijnschilders* which, when translated literally means 'fine painters'. His technical refinement is shown here, for instance, in the fact that some of the tiny letters of the book on the woman's lap are legible enough to suggest that it is devotional in character.

Still life was recognized for the first time as a subject in its own right in the 17th-century Dutch republic. The reason for this can be attributed at least in part to the more comfortable way of life which could be enjoyed after the hardships of the wars of the previous century. Banquet pieces and floral paintings became especially popular, and in

Amsterdam Willem Kalf (1619-1693) developed the so-called *pronk* still life, which mainly represents items of gold, silver, glass and Oriental or Dutch ceramics [10]. The backgrounds of his pictures are usually dark, allowing the precious objects to shimmer and gleam, suggesting a feeling of mystery similar to that found in the works of Rembrandt. Kalf was acknowledged as a master by his contemporaries, in contrast to Abraham van Beyeren (1620/21-1690) whose pictures fetched very low prices during his lifetime. Paintings by both artists are much sought after today, and van Beyeren's *Still life with fish* [11] is a stunning illustration of the Dutch painters' gift for finding material for their art in the most unpromising subjects.

11. *Abraham van Beyeren (1620/21-1690)* Still life with fish, *canvas 99.4 × 125cm (39¼ × 49¼in).*

12. *Jan van Goyen (1596-1656)* Cottages and fishermen by a river, *1631, wood 29.2 × 45.7cm (11½ × 18in).*

13. *Jacob Isaacksz van Ruisdael
(1628/9-1682)* A view of Egmond aan Zee,
late 1640s, wood 49.8 × 68.3cm (19⅝ × 26⅞in).

Flemish landscape painting in the 16th century had tended to be a mixture of fantasy and nature, but, in the early years of the 17th century, Dutch artists began to look at the countryside with a fresh vision. One of the first to do so was Jan van Goyen (1596-1656), who repeatedly travelled up and down the rivers and streams of Holland in search of material for his art. In *Cottages and fishermen by a river* [12] he was attracted as much by the ramshackle signs of man's presence as by the damp vegetation of the river bank, and both elements are brought into a perfectly natural relationship with each other by the unified light and muted colours.

Such a direct response to nature was rare at the time, exerting an influence on the next generation of landscapists, of whom the greatest was Jacob van Ruisdael (1628/9-1682). In *A view of Egmond aan Zee* [13] the artist responds to the fleeting and dramatic light effects of a cloudy morning or evening. The polished technique of another famous landscape painter, Philips Wouwerman (1619-1668), can be seen in *Hawking* [14], with its acutely observed little figures and amazingly clear blue sky.

A very different kind of landscape was painted by Nicolaes Berchem (1620-1683), who was initially a pupil of Jan van Goyen but who turned in later life to Italianate scenes bathed in golden light, a theme which remained immensely popular for over two centuries. It

14. *Philips Wouwerman (1619-1668)*
Hawking, *wood 31.7 × 45.1cm (12½ × 17¾in).*

15. *Nicolaes Pietersz Berchem (1620-1683)*
A country gathering by a bridge, *canvas*
73.3 × 98.7cm (28⅞ × 38⅞in).

has not been established whether or not Berchem actually visited Italy, although the southern atmosphere of such paintings as *A country gathering by a bridge* [15] suggests that he did. Frederik de Moucheron (1633-1686), an Amsterdam painter who worked in a similar vein, spent some years in Italy and produced upon his return many convincingly naturalistic views of the Roman Campagna [16].

The austere interiors of Dutch churches inspired Pieter Jansz Saenredam (1597-1665) to paint some of the most accurately observed and evocative pictures of the 17th century [17]. Their bare walls are reminders of the religious crisis of the previous century, when many sacred works of art were destroyed and the commissioning of new images was contrary to Calvinist beliefs. A few religious pictures were, however, painted for private patrons by artists whose real interests usually lay in other directions. Aelbert Cuyp (1620-1691) was primarily a painter of landscapes with cattle and figures, but the feeling of calm which permeated these also lent itself well to a Biblical subject in *Christ riding into Jerusalem* [18]. Jacob van Loo (1614-1670) was noted as a portraitist and as a painter of mythological, alle-

16. *Frederik de Moucheron (1633-1686)*
Landscape with a ruined tower and figures,
canvas 66 × 77.1cm (26 × 30¼in).

17. *Pieter Jansz Saenredam (1597-1665)*
Interior of the church of St Bavo, Haarlem,
1633, wood 42.8 × 33.6cm (16⅞ × 13¼in).

18. *Aelbert Cuyp (1620-1691)* Christ riding into Jerusalem, *wood 70.8 × 90.8cm (27⅞ × 35¾in).*

gorical and genre scenes. He was also a gifted painter of the nude, as is shown by his *Susanna and the elders* [19], which illustrates the scene of attempted seduction in the Apocryphal story of Susanna.

Rembrandt Harmensz van Rijn (1606-1669) reacted against Dutch 17th-century art's fundamental aim of describing the world from the outside. His work displayed a penetrating insight into humanity, or, as the French 19th century critic Emile Michele wrote, 'he wanted . . . to express in the visible, that which by its very nature is non-material and undefinable'. The fact that he never showed any inclination to specialize in one type of subject is another indication of the enormity of the gap which separated him from most of his contemporaries, and he became by far the most imaginative and versatile painter of the whole century.

Although he was born in Leiden, Rembrandt spent the major part of his career in Amsterdam. In the 1630s he achieved considerable success as a society portraitist and as a painter of official commissions, but his curiosity about the visual world also extended to such unconventional subjects as *The carcase of an ox* [21]. At this date his technique was already becoming less detailed, and there is a strong sense that light, both physical and spiritual, was one of his principal objects of interest. His later works tend to become yet more broad in handling and intimate in feeling. *A man in armour* [25] once belonged to the English 18th-century painter Joshua Reynolds, who found it too dark for his own taste. The darkness, however, provides a poignant contrast to the gleaming armour, creating a mysterious ambience of light and shadow which is typical of the late Rembrandt.

In the 18th century, creatively rather a barren period in Dutch art, taste changed, and manual dexterity and detailed brushwork were extolled above all else. As a result, many pictures lacked originality and were merely slavish reworkings of old themes. There were a few

19. *Jacob van Loo (1614-1670)* Susanna and the elders, *canvas 77.5 × 65.1cm (30½ × 25⅝in).*

notable exceptions, however, such as the work of Rachel Ruysch (1664-1750) and Jan van Huysum (1682-1749), two of the most sensitive and accomplished Dutch flower painters. Ruysch's *Flowers in a terracotta vase* [20] is a small picture executed with an astonishing precision which brings out the character of each leaf and flower. By way of contrast, van Huysum's *Flowers in a terracotta urn* [22] is on a large scale and much more freely painted, its flowers loosely arranged in rhythmic lines reflecting the Rococo style.

In the second half of the 19th century, a group of Dutch artists, known as The Hague School, found their aesthetic home on the coast and low *polders,* or reclaimed land, near the Hague. Jozef Israëls (1824-1911) began his career as a history painter, until, while staying at Zandvoort in 1855, he became fascinated by the poverty-stricken

20. *Rachel Ruysch (1664-1750)* Flowers in a terracotta vase, *1723, canvas 39.4 × 31.4cm (15½ × 12⅜in).*

21. *Rembrandt Harmensz van Rijn (1606-1669)* The carcase of an ox, *late 1630s, wood 73.3 × 51.7cm (28¾ × 20⅜in).*

22. *Jan van Huysum (1682-1749)* Flowers in a terracotta urn, *1727, canvas 157.5 × 109.2cm (62 × 43in).*

23. *Jozef Israëls (1824-1911)* The frugal meal, *before 1876, canvas 88.9 × 138.7cm (35 × 54⅝in).*

existence led by fishermen and their families. Henceforth he abandoned the academic manner and took to painting scenes of peasant and fisher life in a straightforward, unsentimental style which made a dramatic impact on other artists. Vincent van Gogh, for example, owed a significant debt to Israëls' *The frugal meal* [23] when he painted his great early work *The potato eaters* in 1885, whilst B.J. Blommers (1845-1914) formed a friendship with Israëls that lasted all his life and greatly influenced his artistic development. In *On the dunes* [24] it is striking how Blommers has created a vivid impression of reality by his use of an informal composition, a low-keyed palette and deft brushwork. The style is original, but the close relationship between art and life reiterates one of the essential themes of Dutch and Flemish painting.

24. *Bernardus Johannes Blommers (1845-1914)* On the dunes, *wood 30.8 × 19.7cm (12⅛ × 7¾in).*

25. *Rembrandt Harmensz van Rijn (1606-1669)* A man in armour, *1655, canvas 137.5 × 104.5cm (54⅛ × 41¼in).*

French Painting

The greatest ages of French painting were the 17th and the 19th to early 20th centuries. Earlier artists are scarcely represented in Glasgow, but the collection is rich in works of the latter period.

Easel painting emerged in France in the 15th century, developing partly from the work of book illuminators such as the brothers Limbourg (d. before 1416). A similar love of detail and jewel-like colours is found in the earliest French picture at Kelvingrove, *The Nativity with St Jerome, a pope and a cardinal* [1], painted *c.*1450-1475 by an unknown provincial artist of French or possibly north Italian origin. The only other early French painting in the collection is *St Maurice (*or *St Victor) with a donor* [2] by the Master of Moulins (active *c.*1480-*c.*1500) whose style shows the influence of Flemish Renaissance art. Neither the painter, whose name derives from the town of Moulins in central France where his best-known work, an altarpiece, adorns the cathedral, nor the sitters in Glasgow's panel have been convincingly identified.

1. *Unknown, Franco-Italian (c.1450-1475)*
The Nativity with St Jerome, a pope and a cardinal, *wood 52.2 × 41.8cm (20⅜ × 16⅜in).*

2. *Master of Moulins (active c.1480-1500)*
St Maurice (*or* St Victor) with a donor, *wood 58.4 × 49.5cm (23 × 19¼in).*

In the 17th century a native school of French painting was rapidly established. The country's political power led to internal stability and wealth; all the arts were actively encouraged, and in 1648 the Academy of Painting and Sculpture was founded, an organization which dominated artistic affairs in France for over two hundred years. Two contrasting pictorial styles emerged early in the century: the dramatic, decorative baroque practised by Vouet, Le Brun and their followers; and the restrained, intellectual and classically inspired art of Poussin, Claude and Dughet. Of the classicists only the landscape artist Gaspar Dughet (1615-1675) is represented in Glasgow. Pictures like *Ideal landscape* [4] were not records of actual places but imaginary scenes composed in the studio. The only French Baroque work at Kelvingrove is *The four seasons* [3] by Simon Vouet (1590-1649) who brought the influence of Caravaggio from Rome to Paris in 1627. Painted around that time, this allegory shows the seasons as Flora, Adonis, Ceres and Bacchus.

These two opposing strains, one cerebral and disciplined, the other more emotional and flamboyant, reappeared in the late 18th and early 19th centuries as Neoclassicism and Romanticism. There are no works in the former style at Kelvingrove, but the Romantic characteristics of swirling composition, theatrical gestures, rich broken colours and bold brushwork can be seen in *The expulsion of Adam and Eve from Paradise* [5], which was painted in the studio of the leader of the movement, Eugène Delacroix (1798-1863).

Among the painters of this period who began to turn from classical or fanciful landscapes towards direct observation of nature was Georges Michel (1763-1843) whose powerful, atmospheric pictures of the countryside around Paris form a link between Dutch 17th-century landscapes and the art of the Barbizon School [6].

3. *Simon Vouet (1590-1649)* The four seasons, canvas 140.3 × 129.5cm (55¼ × 51in).

4. *Gaspar Dughet (1615-1675)* Ideal landscape, c.1655-1660, canvas 93.6 × 133cm (36¾ × 52⅜in).

5. *Studio of Eugène Delacroix (1798-1863)*
The expulsion of Adam and Eve from
Paradise, *canvas 136.2 × 105.1cm
(53⅝ × 41⅜in).*

6. *Georges Michel (1763-1843)* Landscape
with cottages, *paper on canvas 78.4 × 99cm
(30¾ × 39in).*

One of the most important landscape painters of the 19th century
was Jean-Baptiste-Camille Corot (1796-1875). Although many of his
early landscapes have classical subjects, they are boldly painted
with a new, refreshingly direct approach to nature. Later, prettily
idealized scenes like *Pastorale — souvenir d'Italie* made Corot
immensely popular but today he is more appreciated for his early
work and for small, lively sketches such as *The woodcutter* [7]. He
also produced a few portraits, among them the pensive, enigmatic
Mademoiselle de Foudras [8].

7. *Jean-Baptiste-Camille Corot (1796-1875)*
The woodcutter, *1865-1870, canvas 49.6 ×
64.8cm (19½ × 25⅝in).*

8. *Jean-Baptiste-Camille Corot (1796-1875)*
Mademoiselle de Foudras, *1872, canvas 88.9*
× *59.3cm (35 × 23⅞in).*

Corot was one of the first to paint at the village of Barbizon on the
edge of the Forest of Fontainebleau, which soon attracted many other
artists, among them Théodore Rousseau (1812-1867) [10] who settled there in 1836. The group which gathered round him became
known as The Barbizon School and included Millet, Diaz, Hervier
[9], Troyon, Dupré and Daubigny, all of whom are represented at Kelvingrove. Under the influence of Dutch landscapists, notably Ruisdael, and inspired also by the Englishmen Constable and Bonington,
the Barbizon painters rejected classical landscape and produced
instead pictures of the countryside, animals and people they saw
around them. They often worked out of doors, and as a result effects

9. *Adolphe Hervier (1818-1879)* Village scene, Barbizon, *wood 12.9 × 30.8cm (5⅛ × 12⅛in).*

of light and weather became increasingly important, especially to Charles Daubigny (1817-1878) whose ability to capture the ever-changing sea and sky can be seen in *Seascape at Villerville* [11].

The most significant member of the Barbizon group was not, however, primarily a landscape painter. Jean-François Millet (1814-1875) [12] was deeply concerned with the lives of the peasants and depicted their struggles against the harshness of their labour and the adversities of nature. His figures, like the pair in *Going to work* [14], have a monumental, almost religious, quality that ennobles them. Millet's Realist subject matter was in line with mid-19th-century radical thinking, which, following the 1830 and 1848 Revolutions, advocated democracy and demanded that art should depict contemporary life rather than the archaic historical or mythological themes still favoured by the Academy.

Many other artists of the period also rejected traditional academic work, among them Gustave Courbet (1819-1877) who tried, in his own words, 'to create a living art'. His uncompromising, thickly painted, Realist figure subjects helped to establish contemporary life as an acceptable subject for art. Courbet also produced portraits, landscapes in the Barbizon tradition and still lifes, of which *Flowers in a basket* [13], a formal piece set up in the manner of the Dutch 17th-century flower painters, is one of the finest.

10. *Théodore Rousseau (1812-1867)* The Forest of Clairbois, *c.1836-1839, canvas 65.4 × 104.1cm (25¾ × 41in).*

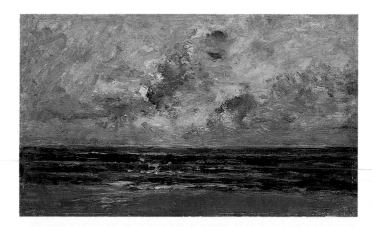

Many 19th-century Realists produced works which, often intentionally, drew attention to the plight of the poor. Among them was Jules Breton (1827-1906) who, in the 1850s, turned from these pictures of misery and despair to seek inspiration in calmer scenes of rural life [15]. Léon Lhermitte (1844-1925) also concentrated on depicting the work of the peasants and became particularly renowned for charcoal drawings such as *The weaver* [16]. Jules Bastien-Lepage (1848-1884), in *Poor Fauvette* [17] and other similar works, tended to sentimentalize his subject matter. A contemporary of the Realists was Henri Fantin-Latour (1836-1904) who, although he is now better known for beautifully observed still lifes [18], attached far greater importance to his elaborate, fanciful paintings inspired by the music of Wagner or Berlioz.

11. *Charles-François Daubigny (1817-1878). Seascape at Villerville, 1876, wood 33 × 56.7cm (13 × 22¼in).*

12. *Jean-François Millet (1814-1875). The sheepfold, 1868, charcoal and pastel 72.1 × 95cm (28¾ × 37¼in).*

13. *Gustave Courbet (1819-1877) Flowers in a basket, 1863, canvas 75.9 × 100.8cm (29⅞ × 39¾in).*

14. *Jean-François Millet (1814-1875) Going to work, 1850-1851, canvas 55.5 × 46cm (21⅞ × 18¼in).*

15. *Jules Breton (1827-1906)* The reapers, *1860, canvas 74.9 × 111.7cm (29¼ × 44in).*

16. *Léon Lhermite (1844-1925)* The weaver, *1882, charcoal 48.9 × 63.2cm (19¼ × 24⅞in).*

In the 1850s and 60s many young artists, like Edouard Manet (1832-1883) — the only major figure of the period not represented at Kelvingrove — followed Courbet in seeking inspiration from modern life but, unlike the Realists, they stressed not the inner significance of the subject but its outward visual aspects. Leader of these younger painters, whose ideas were opposed to and rejected by the Academy, was Claude Monet (1840-1926). The greatest influences on Monet were Barthold Jongkind (1819-1891), a Dutch painter, and Eugène Boudin (1824-1898) who, working out of doors, often on the northern coast of France, produced seascapes and landscapes in which effects of light and weather were emphasized [19].

The group of artists who gathered around Monet in the 1860s came to be known later as the Impressionists. The name, coined as a term of derision by a critic, suited them because their aim was to convey fleeting visual impressions in particular the play of light on landscape. Even their early works, like *The towpath* [20] painted by Camille Pissarro (1830-1903) in 1864, although close in style and concept to the Barbizon landscapes which they admired, show the younger artists' greater preoccupation with light.

17. *Jules Bastien-Lepage (1848-1884)* Poor Fauvette, *1881, canvas 162.5 × 125.7cm (64 × 49½in).*

18. *Henri Fantin-Latour (1836-1904)* Chrysanthemums, *1879, canvas 61 × 48.3cm (24 × 19in).*

19. *Eugène Boudin (1824-1898)* The Port of Deauville, *c.1880-1884, canvas 41 × 53.2cm (16¼ × 21¼in).*

The leading Impressionists were Monet, Pissarro, Sisley, Renoir and Degas, who are all represented at Kelvingrove. Monet was totally absorbed in the movement of light and he nearly always painted landscapes out of doors, often producing series of pictures depicting the same scene at different times of day. Of necessity working rapidly, his technique became bolder and he developed the comma brushstroke which can be seen clearly in *Vétheuil* [21]. He abandoned the use of black and instead painted shadows, such as those in the foreground of *View of Ventimiglia* [22], with a vibrant mixture of blues, greens, purples and even gold.

20. *Camille Pissarro (1830-1903)* The towpath, *1864, canvas 81.9 × 107.9cm (32¼ × 42½in).*

21. *Claude Monet (1840-1926)* Vétheuil, *c.1880, canvas 59.7 × 80cm (23½ × 31½in).*

22. *Claude Monet (1840-1926)* View of Ventimiglia, *1884, canvas 65.1 × 91.7cm (25¾ × 36¼in).*

Of all the Impressionists, it was Alfred Sisley (1839-1899), a painter of English descent, who remained most faithful to their original ideals and continued to paint naturalistic landscapes almost exclusively [23]. Pissarro became dissatisfied for a time with the limitations of Impressionism and, seeking a more formal order in his paintings, became an adherent of Divisionism in the 1880s. He returned to the earlier style, however, in late works like *The Tuileries Gardens* [24], painted in 1900.

Others of the group, notably Auguste Renoir (1841-1919) and Edgar Degas (1834-1917), found the emphasis on landscape and the lack of interest in form too restricting as they placed greater importance on figure painting. Trained in the classical tradition of drawing, Degas' subject matter was almost exclusively the human figure. He was fascinated by unusual poses and his favourite themes were the ballet, women bathing and the racecourse. Degas revolutionized composition by abandoning accepted methods and by turning

23. *Alfred Sisley (1839-1899)* Boatyard at Saint-Mammes, *c.1886, canvas 38.1 × 55.8cm (15 × 22in).*

24. *Camille Pissarro (1830-1903)* The Tuileries Gardens, *1900, canvas 73.6 × 92.3cm (29 × 36¼in).*

25. *Edgar Degas (1834-1917)* Dancers on a bench, c.*1898, pastel 53.7 × 75.6cm (21¼ × 29¾in).*

instead to Japanese prints and photography for inspiration. As a result, his pictures, like the pastel *Dancers on a bench* [25], have unusual, off-centre arrangements. The American-born Mary Cassatt (1844-1926), another Impressionist figure painter, was similarly influenced and produced strong, sensitive studies of mothers and children [26].

In the 1880s many of the next generation, although they were at first adherents of Impressionism, began to react against its preoccupation with spontaneity and purely visual effects. Led by Georges Seurat (1859-1891), the group, known as the Divisionists or Neo-Impressionists, returned to formally organized pictures while at the same time taking the interest in light even farther. Seurat, along with Paul Signac (1863-1935) and others, studied scientific colour theories and evolved a laborious technique which consisted of juxtaposing tiny points of pure colour on the canvas — when viewed from the correct distance the dots appear to merge. Seurat painted a number of huge, classically balanced figure compositions which he carried out in the studio from preparatory studies and sketches. One such sketch is

26. *Mary Cassatt (1844-1926)* The sisters, c.*1885, canvas 46.3 × 55.5cm (18¼ × 21¼in).*

27. *Georges Seurat (1859-1891)* The riverbanks, c.*1883, wood 15.9 × 25.1cm (6¼ × 9⅞in).*

28. *Paul Signac (1863-1935)* Coal-crane,
Clichy, *1884, canvas 59 × 91.4cm
(23¼ × 36in).*

29. *Paul Cézanne (1839-1906)* Overturned
basket of fruit, c.1877, canvas 16 × 32.3cm
(6¼ × 12¾in).

The river-banks [27] which was produced in 1883 for *Une Baignade, Asnières,* now in the National Gallery, London. Signac's *Coal-crane, Clichy* [28] is an interesting transitional work which shows the artist's early Impressionist style giving way to Divisionist brushwork in the foreground. The gallery's other picture by Signac, *Sunset at Herblay* [30], painted in 1889-1890, shows the fully developed dot technique sometimes known as pointillism.

The three greatest figures of late 19th-century Post-Impressionism were Cézanne, Van Gogh and Gauguin. In various ways they all stressed the emotional significance underlying the subject as well as the painting's importance as an object in its own right rather than as merely a pictorial method of recording a scene or conveying a message. This was the beginning of the theory of art for art's sake which lies at the roots of modernism.

Influenced by Courbet and by the classical approach to drawing and form, Paul Cézanne (1839-1906) sought to emphasize the permanence and solidity of the various elements in his pictures. By using the same thick, squarish brushstrokes throughout each canvas and by reducing the contrasts of aerial perspective he unified people and objects with their surroundings so that the whole picture surface became a mass of near-geometric forms. This approach can be seen in the small but powerful *Overturned basket of fruit* [29].

30. *Paul Signac (1863-1935)* Sunset at
Herblay, *1889-1890, canvas 57.1 × 90.2cm
(22½ × 35½in).*

31. *Vincent van Gogh (1853-1890)* Le Moulin
de Blute-Fin, *1886, canvas 45.4 × 37.5cm
(17¾ × 14¾in).*

Vincent van Gogh (1853-1890), a painter of Dutch birth, at first
worked in a dark style akin to that of Israëls and the Hague School,
but after he arrived in Paris in 1886 his palette lightened dramatically
under the influence of Impressionism, as can be seen clearly in *Le
Moulin de Blute-Fin* [31]. The following year he was attracted to Divisionism, and his *Portrait of Alexander Reid* (see pages 99 and 100) was
painted during this phase. He went on to produce his most powerful
and expressive work during the last few years of his life.

The influence of Impressionism is also evident in the early works of
Paul Gauguin (1848-1903). *Oestervold Park, Copenhagen* [32] was
produced in 1885, shortly after he had abandoned a successful business career in Paris in order to paint full time. Inspired by Japanese
prints and by the exotic colours and primitive art which he first discovered on a trip to Martinique in 1887, Gauguin's work became both
more decorative and more symbolic. Emile Bernard (1868-1941) was
one of the group which, for a few years from 1886, gathered around
Gauguin at Pont-Aven, an artists' colony in Brittany. They evolved
the style known as Synthetism, in which forms and colours were sim-
plified for the sake of more forceful expression. Its characteristic flat

32. *Paul Gauguin (1848-1903)* Oestervold
Park, Copenhagen, 1885, canvas 59.1 ×
72.7cm (23¼ × 28⅝in).

33. *Emile Bernard (1868-1941)* Landscape,
Saint-Briac, 1889, canvas 53.9 × 64.1cm
(21¼ × 25¼in).

areas of bright colour separated by dark outlines can be seen in
Bernard's *Landscape, Saint-Briac* [33] of 1889.

Linked stylistically with this kind of Symbolism was the work of the
Nabis, a term derived from the Hebrew word for prophet, who, led by
Pierre Bonnard (1867-1947) and Edouard Vuillard (1868-1940), further developed the idea of the painting as a two-dimensional arrangement of patterns and colours. In many of his pictures, like *Mother and
child* [34], Vuillard intentionally subordinated individual elements to
the overall design. Another picture in the manner of the Nabis is *The
flower seller* [35], which was painted in Paris in 1901 by the Spanish-
born artist Pablo Picasso (1881-1973) before he developed the style
known as Cubism.

34. *Edouard Vuillard (1868-1940)* Mother and
child, c.1899, cardboard 48.6 × 56.5cm (19⅛ ×
22¼in).

35. *Pablo Picasso (1881-1973)* The flower seller, *1901, millboard 33.7 × 52.1cm (13¼ × 20½in).*

36. *Charles Camoin (1879-1965)* Place de Clichy, Paris, *c.1907, canvas 65.1 × 81.3cm (25⅝ × 32in).*

In the early years of the 20th century emotional and intellectual styles were again contrasted in the work of two revolutionary groups, the Fauves and the Cubists. The former, led by Henri Matisse, André Derain and Maurice de Vlaminck, were predominantly interested in colour both for its pictorial value and as a means of expression. They dispensed with the illusion of space and built up their vivid paintings with large flat brush strokes of brilliant colour. Derain (1880-1954), who painted *Blackfriars* [37] around 1906, later said that at that time 'colour became charges of dynamite'. Most of the Fauves (the word means 'wild beasts') are represented at Kelvingrove, although only the Derain and *Place de Clichy, Paris* [36] by Charles Camoin (1879-

37. *André Derain (1880-1954)* Blackfriars, *c.1906, canvas 80.6 × 99.3cm (31¾ × 39¼in).*

38. *Henri Matisse (1869-1954)* Head of a young girl, c.*1919, canvas on cardboard 40.8 × 32.7cm (16¼ × 12⅞in).*

39. *Juan Gris (1887-1927)* The glass, *1918, canvas 26.7 × 15.9cm (10½ × 6¼in).*

40. *Georges Braque (1882-1963)* Still life, *1926, wood 44 × 54.6cm (17¼ × 21½in).*

1965) date from the vital early period of 1905 to 1907. The work of Henri Matisse (1869-1954) later became more formal and decorative, as can be seen in both *The pink tablecloth* and *Head of a young girl* [38]. The latter is related to a larger composition *The black table*, now in Switzerland in a private collection. This work was also painted in 1919.

Cubism was developed by Georges Braque (1882-1963) and Pablo Picasso between 1906 and 1908. Much influenced by Cézanne and by primitive African art, the Cubists, as the name implies, emphasized geometric forms in their work. Kelvingrove's Cubist pictures all belong to the second phase of the movement, known as Synthetic Cubism, when the artists built up images on the canvas using separate shapes, some of which were stuck on rather than painted, in the technique known as collage. During this period others joined the group, including Louis Marcoussis (1878-1941) and the Spaniard Juan Gris (1887-1927) whose still life *The glass* [39] of 1918 is a typical Synthetic Cubist work. The Gallery's paintings by Marcoussis and Braque [40], which are the most recent French pictures in the collection, date from the 1920s, by which time Cubism had lost impetus and become more decorative.

British Painting
(artists born before 1850)

Paintings by Scottish artists predominate in the British collections at Kelvingrove, but, particularly in the period before 1850, there are sufficient characteristic examples by their English contemporaries to allow a gallery arrangement which shows the development of Scottish painting within the British school. Throughout the 17th century and for most of the 18th, apart from some decorative painting, portraiture was the only category which guaranteed a secure living for the professional artist in Britain, and London was the centre of fashionable patronage. Aspiring Scottish artists were advised to leave home to complete their training, usually in Italy. Those with sufficient talent and ambition settled in London or abroad to establish a reputation.

There are few Scottish 17th-century portrait painters of merit; George Jamesone (1589/90-1644), an example of whose work is at Kelvingrove on loan from a private collection, is the most significant, but his work must be judged as provincial when compared with the great names of the London art scene — Van Dyck, Lely and Kneller. Jamesone's near contemporary, the London-based painter Gerard Soest (*c.*1600-1681), was a popular choice for sitters who wanted a

1. *Gerard Soest (c.1600-1681)* John Hay, 2nd Marquis of Tweeddale, *c.1670, canvas 125.9 × 105.2cm (49⅝ × 41¼in).*

2. *John Michael Wright (1617-1694)* Frances, daughter of Oliver Cromwell, *c.1658, canvas 101.5 × 112cm (40 × 43¾in).*

3. *William Gouw Ferguson (c.1632- c.1695)* Still life, *1690, canvas 59.1 × 48.3cm (23¼ × 19in).*

good quality portrait but at a lower price than that charged by Sir Peter Lely, the leading court painter of the time. Soest's attractive portrait of the *2nd Marquis of Tweeddale* as a young man [1] shows him dressed in Eastern fashion. The practice of painting sitters in unusual garments originated at the court of Elizabeth I of England where exotic costume was worn at masques. In the 17th and 18th centuries, concern that portraits should not become dated often led to sitters being depicted in fancy dress, in classical draperies or, as in many of Lely's compositions, in simple loose-fitting shifts. However, John Michael Wright (1617-1694), one-time apprentice of George Jamesone but a far more sophisticated artist, painted Frances, the recently widowed and soon to be remarried daughter of Oliver Cromwell, in fashionable dress [2]. In this portrait, elements of still life are present in the objects symbolic of her bereaved state, but there was little demand for the type of pure still life by the Scottish artist William Gouw Ferguson (*c*.1632-*c*.1695) [3]. He spent most of his life in Holland and his work belongs to the northern European tradition.

In the 18th century the portrait painter William Aikman (1682-1731) was one of the first Scots to achieve success in London. His picture, *John Dalrymple, 2nd Earl of Stair* [4], which bears a later inscription incorrectly identifying the sitter as the 2nd Duke of Argyll, is typical of commissions carried out for members of the Scottish nobility. Aikman was an accomplished and sensitive painter whose sitters probably appreciated his tendency to smooth out irregularities in their features, which gave his portraits an aristocratic elegance. More informal was the work of Scottish-born Gawen Hamilton (1697-1737) [5] who, by the early 1730s, had established himself in London as a painter of conversation pieces. This type of small group portrait, showing people in a domestic setting, became popular in Britain in the early 18th century. Several major painters, notably William Hogarth, launched their careers as conversation-piece artists and at the time, Hamilton, although more limited in artistic ability, was regarded as a rival to Hogarth. A later and more sophisticated conversation piece, *A family party — the minuet* [6], entered the collection in 1854 with an attribution to Johann Zoffany

4. *William Aikman (1682-1731)* John Dalrymple, 2nd Earl of Stair, c.1727, canvas 128.2 × 99.7cm (48¼ × 39¼in).

5. *Gawen Hamilton (1697-1737)* The vicar of the parish visits the infant squire, c.1730, canvas 74.9 × 94.6cm (29½ × 37¼in).

6. *Johann Zoffany (1733-1810)* A family party — the minuet, c.1780, canvas 99.1 × 124.5cm (39 × 49in).

7. *Allan Ramsay (1713-1784)* Henrietta Diana, Dowager Countess of Stafford, *1759, canvas 94.6 × 73.7cm (31½ × 29in).*

8. *Gavin Hamilton (1723-1798)* Apollo and Artemis, *c.1770, canvas 170.3 × 120cm (67 × 47¼in).*

(1733-1810). This has been doubted on stylistic grounds but so far no convincing alternative has been suggested.

Allan Ramsay (1713-1784), a man of outstanding artistic and intellectual ability, followed Hogarth as a leading portrait painter in London in the middle of the 18th century. Ramsay's portrait of *Henrietta Diana, Dowager Countess of Stafford* [7] is an example of the artist's mature style, where the sensitive exploration of character and the atmospheric qualities of light have replaced an earlier, more robust manner. The son of Allan Ramsay the poet, Ramsay studied in London and Italy before setting up as a portrait painter in London in 1738. He retained a house and studio in his native Edinburgh, to which he frequently returned to carry out commissions and to renew contact with his friends. Ramsay abandoned painting in the early 1770s, perhaps because of a serious injury to his right arm, and devoted himself to literary and philosophical pursuits.

Of all the 18th-century Neoclassical designers in Britain, Josiah Wedgwood, the pottery manufacturer, and Robert Adam, the Scottish architect, are probably the best known and were amongst the most influential, but on the Continent two Scottish painters achieved equal prominence. Gavin Hamilton (1723-1798), theorist, antiquarian and artist, was one of the founders of the European Neoclassical movement. A graduate of Glasgow University, he studied painting in Italy and settled in Rome in the late 1750s, producing a series of vast canvases compared to which his *Apollo and Artemis* [8] is small. Most of Hamilton's subjects were taken from Greek history and literature, and his paintings were intended to inspire noble thoughts. In Neoclassical landscape painting, the ambitious compositions of Jacob More (1740-1793) were highly regarded, Sir Joshua Reynolds considering him 'the best painter of air since Claude'. *Morning* and *Evening* [9], the two landscapes in the Gallery's collection, were painted in Rome in 1785 and were admired by the great German writer Goethe, who visited More's studio in 1787.

9. *Jacob More (1740-1793)* Evening, *1785, canvas 152.2 × 203cm (60 × 80in).*

A third Scot who spent some years in Italy, David Allan (1744-1796) is an artist particularly relevant to Glasgow, for he was one of the first and most talented of the pupils at the Foulis Academy of the Fine Arts which was founded in 1753 at the city's College, now the University. The Academy's proprietors, the brothers Robert and Andrew Foulis, followed the European practice of sending their best pupils to Rome to complete their studies. Allan went there under the patronage of the Cathcart family and was drawn into the field of history painting. His *Vestals attending the sacred fire* [10], painted in Rome in 1772, was shown in London after his return to Britain, but Allan found little demand for history painting at home and thereafter concentrated on portraiture, conversation pieces and genre. His most original contribution to the development of Scottish painting lay in his drawings of everyday life — themes which were to be further explored by Sir David Wilkie and his followers in the 19th century.

Meanwhile, Ramsay's pupil and assistant at his London studio, David Martin (1737-1797), returned home to Edinburgh where he

10. *David Allan (1744-1796)* The vestals attending the sacred fire, *1772, canvas 147.6 × 174cm (58¼ × 68½in).*

11. *David Martin (1737-1797)* George Murdoch, *1793, canvas 91.4 × 71.1cm (36 × 28in).*

12. *Henry Raeburn (1756-1823)* Mr and Mrs Robert Campbell of Kailzie *canvas 241.3 × 152.4cm (95 × 60in).*

made a good living as a portraitist towards the end of the century at a time when the city was emerging as a centre of commerce and learning. His sitters included aristocrats and prominent public figures. One of these was *George Murdoch* [11], a merchant engaged in trade with Madeira and twice Lord Provost of Glasgow.

Martin encouraged the young Henry Raeburn (1756-1823), who was to become the first Scottish portrait painter of international stature to remain in his own country for most of his professional life. Raeburn's outstanding gift was his ability to convey the personality of his subject with a few apparently effortless brush strokes. He was admired for this by his English rival, Sir Thomas Lawrence, who remarked 'Mr Raeburn's style is freedom itself'. This quality is particularly evident in the double portrait of *Mr and Mrs Robert Campbell of Kailzie* [12], in which the dramatic lighting, the boldly sketched landscape setting and the sense of the fleeting moment firmly place Raeburn amongst the Romantics.

Landscapes of actual places began to find a market towards the middle of the 18th century as interest in the natural scenery of the British Isles became fashionable. In Scotland, landscape painting had its beginnings in the work of decorative painters such as the Norie family of Edinburgh [13], and was established as a respectable branch of the fine arts by Alexander Nasmyth (1758-1840). Nasmyth, like David Martin, worked for a while in London as one of Ramsay's assistants, studied in Italy and subsequently set up a school teaching landscape painting both to professional artists and to amateurs, helped by his large and talented family. From the astonishing variety of Scottish scenery Alexander Nasmyth [14] chose to paint the picturesque: crumbling ruins, serene lochs framed by tall trees, and mountains bathed in rosy light.

Nasmyth's interest in the changing effects of light and weather was developed by the next generation — John Knox and the Rev. John Thomson in Scotland and by the two giants of landscape painting in England, J.M.W. Turner (1775-1851) and John Constable (1776-1837). The latter two are each represented in the collection by

13. *James Norie (1684-1757)* Landscape with rustics and sheep near a castle *canvas* 118 × 92cm (46¼ × 36¼in).

14. *Alexander Nasmyth (1758-1840)* A rocky wooded landscape, 1817, *canvas* 78.1 × 115.5cm (30¾ × 45½in).

a major work: Turner by *Modern Italy — the Pifferari* [15], which was first owned by a Scot, H.A.J. Munro of Novar, a personal friend and patron of Turner; and Constable by *Hampstead Heath* [17], one of the artist's many paintings of this locality.

The Glasgow landscape painter John Knox (1778-1845) produced picturesque views of the West of Scotland. *First steamboat on the Clyde* shows the view looking down the river from Dalnottar Hill [18], a scene repeatedly painted by Knox himself, by his pupils and by numerous later artists. His most successful pupil was Horatio McCulloch (1805-1867), whose *Glencoe* [19] typifies the artist at the height of his popularity as a painter of the grander aspects of the Scottish landscape. His great achievement was to convey his reaction to Scotland's often bleak mountain scenery and erratic weather in a manner which found acceptance amongst his patrons, the rich merchants of Glasgow. The Glasgow portrait painter Daniel Macnee (1806-1882) chose to depict his friend Horatio sketching out of doors in a stormy Highland landscape [16]. It was McCulloch's practice to spend the summer months making on-the-spot studies in oil and watercolour which were the basis for his finished exhibition pieces.

Atmospheric effects preoccupied McCulloch's successors, of whom there were many in the latter part of the century. William McTaggart (1835-1910) [20], the most original and influential, may have seen the work of French contemporaries, and developed his own kind of Impressionism, although his painting is as much in the tradition of Constable in its concern with flickering light and stormy skies.

15. *J.M.W. Turner (1775-1851)* Modern Italy — the Pifferari, *1838, canvas 92.6 × 123.2cm (36½ × 48½in).*

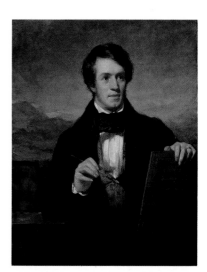

16. *Daniel Macnee (1806-1882)* Horatio McCulloch, *c.1840, canvas 91.4 × 71.1cm (36 × 28in).*

17. *John Constable (1776-1837)* Hampstead Heath, *c.1830, canvas 66.3 × 99.1cm (26¼ × 39in).*

18. *John Knox (1778-1845)* First steamboat on the Clyde, *c.1820, canvas 111.8 × 158.5cm (44 × 62⅜in).*

Whilst early Scottish landscapists were, and still are, virtually unknown outside their own country, David Wilkie (1785-1841) achieved tremendous popularity in England and abroad with his paintings of Scottish village life [21]. In 1805 Wilkie felt obliged to move to London to find patronage, and his reputation was quickly made there. His early work was inspired by Dutch 17th-century genre painting, but following travels in Italy and Spain he later broadened his style and adopted a wider range of subject matter.

By the middle of the 19th century, to remain in Scotland was at last a reasonably attractive financial prospect for the professional artist. There were opportunities to exhibit both in Edinburgh and Glasgow. The Trustees Academy in Edinburgh, founded in 1760 as a training school for industrial designers, had become more attuned to the needs of the student of painting. The intense cultural life of the city, which had emerged in the early years of the century, was maintained but even so many Scottish artists felt the need to settle in London for at least part of their careers. Today it is the names of these exiles that are best known for they belong to the various London-based art movements of the 19th century: William Dyce, Sir William Quiller Orchardson and John Pettie are notable examples. Those who remained in Scotland — James Drummond, Sir George Harvey, Thomas Duncan and many more — can be justifiably labelled as Scottish school. The techniques taught at the Trustees Academy separated Scottish-trained artists stylistically from their English contemporar-

19. *Horatio McCulloch (1805-1867)* Glencoe, *1864, canvas 110.5 × 182.9cm (43¼ × 72in).*

20. *William McTaggart (1835-1910)* The Paps of Jura, *1902, canvas 137.5 × 208.3cm (54¼ × 82in).*

21. *David Wilkie (1785-1841)* The cottar's Saturday night, *1837, panel 83.8 × 108cm (33 × 42¼in).*

22. *George Harvey (1806-1876)* The Covenanters' preaching, *c.1830, panel 82.6 × 106.7cm (32¼ × 42in).*

ies, and their shared preference for subjects from Scottish history, literature and everyday life is conspicuous. In *The Covenanters' preaching* [22] Sir George Harvey (1806-1876) looks back in a somewhat sentimental way to the religious conflicts of the 17th century whilst Robert Herdman (1829-1888) glamorizes the past by presenting the ageing Mary, Queen of Scots as a young and beautiful woman, the innocent victim of political intrigue [23]. In contrast, the pathos expressed in *The last of the clan* [24] by Thomas Faed (1826-1900) is a truthful and heartfelt reaction to a very recent tragedy, the enforced emigration resulting from the Highland Clearances.

23. *Robert Herdman (1829-1888)* Execution
of Mary, Queen of Scots, *1867, canvas
74.9 × 95.3cm (29¼ × 37½in).*

24. *Thomas Faed (1826-1900)* The last of
the clan, *1865, canvas 144.8 × 182.9cm
(57 × 72in).*

Those Scottish painters whose subject matter was generally out-side the confines of nationalism are significant too and are perhaps a necessary antidote to the accusations of provincialism sometimes levelled at the Scottish historical and genre school. David Scott (1806-1849) spent most of his life in Edinburgh yet he painted grand and imaginative subjects in the tradition of James Barry and William Blake — the Gallery's large oil, *Nimrod* [25], represents him as a romantic and a visionary. Other Scottish artists made their reputa-tions through work resulting from foreign travel — David Roberts (1796-1864) with Spanish and Middle Eastern landscape subjects and John Phillip (1817-1867) with his exotic scenes of everyday life in Spain.

David Scott's brother, William Bell Scott (1811-1890), provides a link between Scottish art and the Pre-Raphaelite Brotherhood in England. After training in Edinburgh, Bell Scott moved to England where he became a lifelong friend of Dante Gabriel Rossetti (1828-1882), who is represented in the collection by *Regina Cordium: Alice Wilding* [26]. Bell Scott's *Fair Rosamond alone in her bower* [28], which was first exhibited in 1853, is a painting in which the artist emulates Pre-Raphaelite technique, depicting natural objects in

25. *David Scott (1806-1849)* Nimrod, *c.1832, canvas 177.8 × 140.3cm (70 × 55¼in).*

26. *Dante Gabriel Rossetti (1828-1882)* Regina Cordium: Alice Wilding, *1866, canvas 59.7 × 49.5cm (23¼ × 19¼in).*

27. *William Dyce (1806-1864)* Christabel, *1855, panel 54 × 44.8cm (21¼ × 17⅝in).*

minute detail and brilliant colours, and also adopts the kind of romantic literary subject popular with The Brotherhood. The Aberdonian William Dyce (1806-1864) belongs even more than Bell Scott to the mainstream of British painting. He was a leader of the revival of fresco painting in London, an influential teacher and one of the first to recognize the merits of the Pre-Raphaelites. His *Christabel* [27] harmonizes well with paintings by Rossetti, Ford Madox Brown and Burne-Jones and with the work of his fellow Scot, Joseph Noel Paton (1821-1901), which in technique and attention to detail also has much in common with the Pre-Raphaelite Brotherhood [29].

Glasgow's Burne-Jones is one of the gems of the collection. *Danaë* or *The tower of brass* [33], the artist's third and largest version of the subject, depicts Danaë, the daughter of Acrisius, King of Argos, watching the building of a brazen tower in which her father intends to imprison her. To the artist, however, the details of the legend were unimportant. Edward Burne-Jones (1833-1898) belonged to the second phase of Pre-Raphaelitism. He was not concerned with storytelling nor with moralizing. He said that his intention was to create 'a beautiful romantic dream of something that never was, never will be — in a light better than any light that ever shone — in a land no one can define or remember, only desire. . . .'

Near contemporaries of Burne-Jones were two Scottish artists who were successful in London with paintings of a quite different kind. Having trained in Edinburgh at the Trustees Academy under Robert Scott Lauder, William Quiller Orchardson (1835-1910) and John Pettie (1839-1893) moved to London together in 1862, where they shared a house in Pimlico with fellow Edinburgh student, Tom Graham. Both artists began by specializing in historical costume genre, which proved popular with their largely middle-class patrons.

28. *William Bell Scott (1811-1890)* Fair Rosamond alone in her bower, c.1853, canvas 68 × 51.4cm (26¾ × 20¼in).

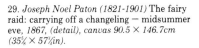

29. *Joseph Noel Paton (1821-1901)* The fairy raid: carrying off a changeling — midsummer eve, 1867, (detail), canvas 90.5 × 146.7cm (35¾ × 57¾in).

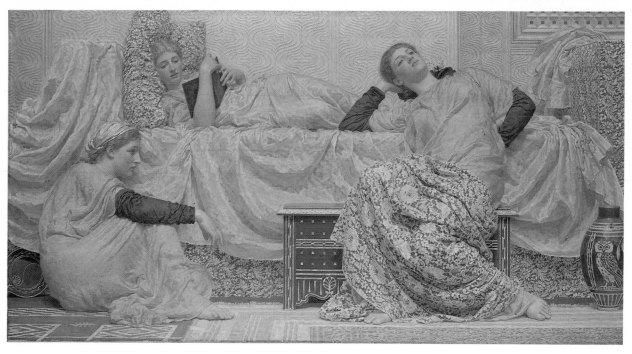

Indeed, Pettie seldom depicted his characters in modern dress: the three young people in his *Two strings to her bow* [30] are in Regency costume which, together with the sentimental subject, perhaps distracts from Pettie's considerable skill as a colourist. Orchardson did paint contemporary scenes, of which *Le mariage de convenance* [31], and its sequel in Aberdeen Art Gallery, are amongst the best known. Here the theme of domestic misery is more subtly expressed than is Pettie's more frivolous fiction. Whilst his subjects appealed to popular taste, Orchardson's excellence as a draughtsman and painter was admired by such opponents of the anecdotal as Sickert and Whistler. The latter also admired and was influenced by the work of Albert Moore (1841-1893) whose *Reading aloud* [32] is a typical example of the artist's 'faint, flower-tinged harmonies'. The carefully balanced tonal composition anticipates the kind of effect achieved by Whistler in his *Nocturnes* and *Arrangements*.

30. *John Pettie (1839-1893)* Two strings to her bow, *1887, canvas 84 × 120.8cm (33¼ × 47½in).*

31. *William Quiller Orchardson (1835-1910)* Le mariage de convenance, *1883, canvas 104.8 × 154.3cm (41¼ × 60¾in).*

32. *Albert Moore (1841-1893)* Reading aloud, *1884, canvas 107.3 × 205.7cm (42¼ × 81in).*

33. *Edward Burne-Jones (1833-1898)* Danaë
or The tower of brass, *1887-1888, canvas
231.1 × 113cm (91 × 44¹⁄₄in).*

34. *James A. McN. Whistler (1834-1903)*
Arrangement in grey and black no.2: Portrait
of Thomas Carlyle, *1872-1873, canvas
171.7 × 143.5cm (67⁷⁄₈ × 56¹⁄₄in).*

To many, the most important painting in the British collection is
undoubtedly the portrait of the historian Thomas Carlyle by the
American-born James A. McNeill Whistler (1834-1903), which the
artist entitled *Arrangement in grey and black no. 2: Portrait of Thomas
Carlyle* [34] (*no. 1* was the famous portrait of his mother, now in the
Louvre in Paris). Whistler's choice of titles such as *Arrangement* or
Symphony showed that he had more concern for the visual effects of
shape and colour than for the significance or detailed appearance of
the subject. In his search for overall pictorial harmony, Whistler was
one of the first Western painters to seek inspiration in the unusual
compositional devices and decorative qualities of Japanese art.
Before reaching the final, apparently simple statement of this portrait, he reworked the canvas many times to create the correct balance — it can be seen where he altered the position of the right hand
and the shoulder — and he even used his famous stylized butterfly
'signature', lower right, as an integral element of the composition.
Carlyle was the first work by this most influential artist to enter a
British public collection.

British Painting
(artists born after 1850)

The Whistler portrait of Thomas Carlyle was bought for the gallery in 1891 after strong representations were made to the then Corporation by a group of young artists who became known as The Glasgow Boys, and whose own work is one of the outstanding features of the collection. Born mostly in the late 1850s, they first came together in the early 1880s to form a loosely knit group of around twenty artists. Like their idol, Whistler, they were innovative, anti-establishment and at times severely criticized, especially at home. *Hard at it* [1], by a leading member of the Boys, James Guthrie (1859-1930), was painted out of doors, following the example of the Barbizon School. During several summers Guthrie, John Lavery, James Paterson, George Henry and their friends established artistic colonies in central and lowland Scotland, at Cockburnspath on the east coast, at Rosneath on the Clyde (*Hard at it* was painted at one or other of these spots), at Brig o'Turk in the Trossachs, at Cambuskenneth near Stirling, and at Kirkcudbright in Galloway. In the winter months they retreated to their Glasgow studios to work together. Some had studied in France, where they had seen the work of another of their heroes, Bastien-Lepage, whose version of rustic realism appealed to them as an antidote to the hackneyed Highland views, historicism and anecdotal sentimentality of the Scottish academic painters. There is a straightforward, earthy quality in Guthrie's *Old Willie — the village worthy* [2] and in *The deserter* [3] by William Kennedy (1859-1918). The latter shows the Boys' French-inspired penchant for peasant themes, which had its parallel in England in the work of George Clausen (1852-1944). John Lavery (1856-1941), although born in Ireland, studied at Glasgow School of Art and was drawn to the group by their shared ideals. His

1. *James Guthrie (1859-1930)* Hard at it, *1883, canvas 31.1 × 46cm (12¼ × 18⅛in).*

2. *James Guthrie (1859-1930)* Old Willie — the village worthy, *1886, canvas 60.8 × 50.8cm (24 × 20in).*

3. *William Kennedy (1859-1918)* The deserter, *1886, canvas 88.9 × 152.4cm (35 × 60in).*

Glasgow Exhibition, 1888 [4], one of many lively compositions he painted at this international cultural and industrial extravaganza held in Kelvingrove Park, well illustrates the debt the Boys owed to Whistler. James Paterson (1854-1932) combined a lowland rustic theme with Whistlerian colour harmonies in *The last turning, winter, Moniaive* [5], a placid view of his adopted home town in Dumfriesshire. The block lettering of the signature, inspired by that of Bastien-Lepage, is a feature often repeated in the Boys' work of the 1880s.

A Galloway landscape [6] by George Henry (1858-1943) is seen as a key work of the group. Painted while Henry was staying with Hornel at Kirkcudbright, the grassy knoll ringed by the tracks of the Galloway cattle and covered in scrubby thornbushes is entirely typical of the area; yet the work is far removed from simple topography. This is an exercise in picture-making in which the artist has reworked and altered the canvas many times, building up a surface texture in parts as rich as a Persian carpet, and introducing a meandering blue-black stream, of oriental derivation, which flattens out the whole picture space. The apparently unfinished nature of parts of the picture, in

4. *John Lavery (1856-1941)* Glasgow Exhibition, 1888, *canvas 61 × 45.7cm (24 × 18in).*

5. *James Paterson (1854-1932)* The last turning, winter, Moniaive, *1885, canvas 61.3 × 91.4cm (24⅛ × 36in).*

6. *George Henry (1858-1943)* A Galloway landscape *,1889, canvas 121.9 × 152.4cm (48 × 60in).*

7. *George Henry (1858-1943)* Japanese lady with a fan, *1894, canvas 61 × 40.6cm (24 × 16in).*

which the white clouds have more solidity than the evanescent cattle and bushes on the hillside, confused and enraged critics at the time, but with our present knowledge of Gauguin's style, with which this has an affinity (although it is not known if Henry was aware of his work) and of later abstract art, we can see that he had made an exciting breakthrough which sadly he never developed further.

The most intriguing picture by the Glasgow Boys in the collection is *The Druids — bringing in the mistletoe* [8], a collaboration between Henry and his friend Edward A. Hornel (1864-1933), which was painted in their Glasgow studio. The intense symbolism of the subject, the flattening of the picture space and telescoping of human scale, and the introduction of gold leaf and a Celtic carved frame, are original and striking new elements. It was not in Britain, however, but on the Continent — in Belgium and Austria — that artists were to develop further the strange linear rhythms and mysticism seen in this picture.

Henry and Hornel's next venture was a painting trip to Japan in 1893-1894, financed by the Glasgow dealer Alex Reid. Henry's *Japanese lady with a fan* [7] shows that he responded not only to the exotic costumes but also to the art of the Japanese: the unusual point of view, the creation of beautiful shapes by skilful manipulation of the brush, the simplification of the background, all bear the stamp of the Oriental tradition. Hornel, on the other hand, seems to have been more receptive to the bright colours and lush flora of the east than to the lessons of its art, as is seen in his thickly painted *The fish pool* [9]. This visit marked the high point in the achievement of the Glasgow Boys. Afterwards, many became established artists, with a consequent slackening of pace and loss of vitality.

The Gallery has oil paintings by all of the Boys, including E.A.

8. *George Henry (1858-1943) and Edward A. Hornel (1864-1933)* The Druids — bringing in the mistletoe, *1890, canvas 152.4 × 152.4cm (60 × 60in).*

9. *Edward A. Hornel (1864-1933)* The fish pool, *1894, canvas 45.1 × 35.6cm (17¾ × 14in).*

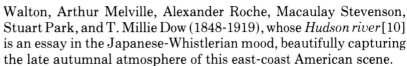

10. *T. Millie Dow (1848-1919)* The Hudson river, *1885, canvas 123.2 × 97.8cm (48¼ × 38½in).*

11. *John Q. Pringle (1864-1925)* Two figures at a fence, *1904, canvas 25.4 × 30.5cm (10 × 12in).*

Walton, Arthur Melville, Alexander Roche, Macaulay Stevenson, Stuart Park, and T. Millie Dow (1848-1919), whose *Hudson river*[10] is an essay in the Japanese-Whistlerian mood, beautifully capturing the late autumnal atmosphere of this east-coast American scene.

Another Glasgow artist active at the same time as the Boys, although not a member of the group, was John Quinton Pringle (1864-1925), who ran an optician's and scientific instrument shop in the city, devoting his spare time to painting and attending classes at the Glasgow School of Art. The microscopic dots of paint in *Two figures at a fence*[11] are a characteristic of his style and reflect the technique of the Neo-Impressionists, which Pringle may have known through his avid study of contemporary art journals. The movement created in this little canvas, which predates the work of the Cubist-inspired Italian Futurists, is, however, quite astonishing and stamps Pringle as a unique and innovative artist.

Another prime feature of the Gallery at Kelvingrove is the work of the Scottish Colourists — Peploe, Cadell, Hunter and Fergusson. The term Colourist, first used of them in 1948 when three were already dead, served to explain their shared love of colour rather than to indicate a coherent group. None originated in Glasgow, but they followed the example of the Boys by seeking inspiration and instruction abroad, particularly in France. J.D. Fergusson (1874-1961), whose early work shows his admiration for Melville and Whistler, settled in France from 1907 to 1914 during which time he produced his most important work strongly influenced by Matisse and the Fauves. *The pink parasol: Bertha Case* [12], painted in Paris in 1908, is a fine example of the current Parisian manner, strong in colour and bold in execution. Later, Fergusson's paintings of naval dockyards at Portsmouth, done at the invitation of the War Memorials Committee in

12. *John D. Fergusson (1874-1961)* The pink parasol: Bertha Case, *1908, millboard 75.2 × 63.5cm (29¾ × 25in).*

1918, afforded him a greater opportunity to show his understanding of Cubism; in *Damaged destroyer* [13] he introduced simple geometric shapes suggested by wharfside constructions.

The early academic training received in Edinburgh and Paris by S.J. Peploe (1871-1935) had little influence. Instead, he learned directly from the work of Manet, Cézanne and the Cubists and also from his close association with Fergusson, with whom he first worked at Paris-Plage on the north coast of France in 1906. The style which he eventually evolved, as seen in *The brown crock* [14], owes most to Cézanne. The dark outlines, the almost geometric simplification of the shapes, and the strong, clear colours made up the formula which he successfully applied to his many still lifes and landscapes.

F.C.B. Cadell (1883-1937) adopted a similar style when working with Peploe on Iona in the 1920s, but moved on to a more personal form of expression, redolent of the fashionable circles in which he moved. *Interior — the orange blind* [15], believed to have been

13. *John D. Fergusson (1874-1961)* **Damaged** destroyer, *1918, canvas 73.6 × 76.2cm (29 × 30in).*

14. *Samuel J. Peploe (1871-1935)* The brown crock, *c.1925, canvas 61 × 50.8cm (24 × 20in).*

15. *Francis C.B. Cadell (1883-1937)* Interior — the orange blind, *c.1928, canvas 111.8 × 86.4cm (44 × 34in).*

painted in his spacious Georgian New Town flat in Edinburgh, captures the flavour of the era and shows to good effect the flat areas of strong colour which this artist favoured.

In contrast to Peploe and Cadell, Leslie Hunter (1877-1931), who was born in Rothesay, was an altogether more Bohemian and financially less successful artist. He painted with great gusto, responding directly to the subject before him. His best work, such as *Old Mill, Fifeshire* [16], vibrates with colour. Whereas Peploe, Cadell and Fergusson at times used the more analytical approach of Cézanne, and to some extent the Cubists, Hunter appears to have been closest to that master of colour, Matisse, whom he certainly admired. Of all four artists, he is most deserving of the title Colourist.

The history of Scottish painting later in the 20th century is more difficult to follow because of the lack of convenient groupings and because we are still too close in time to allow a proper perspective.

William Johnstone (1897-1981), although he spent most of his active life teaching in England, is seen as a highly significant figure in that he was one of the first to paint abstract images. In *Border landscape — the Eildon Hills c.*1929 [17] he used the view of the hills of his native country near Melrose merely as a starting point from which to create an interesting rhythmic pattern of the lines and masses created by dykes, fences and plantations, allied to a rather sombre scheme which interprets a certain mood of Scottish weather. His colours, indeed, are more truly Scottish than those of the Colourists, who painted in what was essentially a Continental manner. Although he had learned much when studying in Paris under André Lhote in 1925 and 1926, Johnstone, being a staunch patriot, sought inspiration in the primitive traditional art of Scotland and Scandinavia, evolving a style which has a mysterious northern European quality.

French art continued to exert an influence on Scots painters in the 1940s and 50s. Robert Colquhoun (1914-1962) and Robert Mac-Bryde (1913-1966) painted in styles strongly influenced by Picasso

16. *Leslie Hunter (1877-1931)* Old Mill, Fifeshire *canvas 50.8 × 68.6cm (20 × 27in).*

and Braque, but also with a flavour of the artists of the English 20th-century Romantic School, such as John Piper (born 1903) and Graham Sutherland. The 'Two Roberts' studied together at Glasgow School of Art but spent most of their later lives together in London, where they designed for the stage as well as painted pictures. Colquhoun's *The lock gate* [18] is an example of their Romantic style, while MacBryde's *The backgammon player* [21] shows the figure distortions found in the work of Picasso.

A different response to French art is evident in the still lifes and landscapes of William Gillies (1898-1973), who studied under André Lhote in Paris in 1924 after graduating from Edinburgh College of Art. *Still life — blue and brown* [19] shows an obvious debt to Braque, but the harshness of Cubism is tempered by Gillies' softer colour harmonies and brushwork. A fascination with colour drew him towards the work of another Frenchman, Bonnard, whose influence is particularly evident in Gillies' landscapes. These two quite distinct styles seem to run in parallel throughout all his work.

Through the thirties, forties and fifties there existed in Scotland a loosely defined school of painters centred on the teaching staff of Edinburgh College of Art, where Gillies became Head of the School of Painting in 1946. The exploitation of the sensuous qualities of oil paint — often known as *belle peinture* —was one of their hallmarks. A good example of this is *Pinks* [20] by Anne Redpath (1895-1965), in which the artist's indulgence in the joy of colour is matched by the generous application of paint — a legacy perhaps of her stay on the Côte d'Azure from 1923 to 1934. Redpath relied more on these qualities and less on line than did Gillies, and at times her work takes on the surface qualities of abstract painting.

17. *William Johnstone (1897-1981)* Border landscape: the Eildon Hills, *c.1929, canvas 71 × 91cm (28 × 35¾in).*

18. *Robert Colquhoun (1914-1962)* The lock gate, *1942, canvas 39 × 58cm (15¼ × 23in).*

19. *William G. Gillies (1898-1973)* Still life —
blue and brown, *1952, canvas 99.1 × 137.2cm
(39 × 54in).*

20. *Anne Redpath (1895-1965)* Pinks, *1947,
canvas 55.9 × 76.2cm (22 × 30in).*

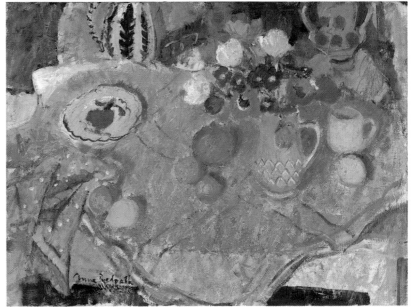

21. *Robert MacBryde (1913-1966)* The
backgammon player, c.*1947, canvas 106.7 ×
76.2cm (42 × 30in).*

Joan Eardley (1921-1963), who is held by many to be the most
important artist in postwar Scotland, was born in Sussex but came to
Glasgow in 1939 and studied at the School of Art. Her two principal
themes are the street urchins of the city and landscapes and seascapes around Catterline, an old fishing village she 'discovered' on the
east coast about 1950. *A stormy sea no. 1* [22] is one of many striking
shoreline compositions she painted *in situ* at Catterline, her easel
weighted down with stones in the teeth of the gale. Her immediate
response to the elements is seen in the bold, often frenzied application
of the paint, owing something to the late work of Turner and also
American Abstract Expressionism which was internationally in
vogue at the time.

A recognizably abstract style was brought to Scottish art by William Gear (born 1915) who was associated with the Cobra Group, founded by Karl Appel in Paris just after the Second World War, and who shared an exhibition in New York with the famous action painter Jackson Pollok. Gear evolved a formal theme of interlaced upright and diagonal shapes, made up of black, white and strong, almost primary colours, of which *Summer garden* [23] is a typical example. Although it had links with international movements in art, Gear's work remained stylistically rather isolated in Scotland.

The Gallery continues to acquire the work of contemporary Scottish artists, the most recent being *Untitled 1984* [24] by Bruce McLean (born 1944). McLean, a Glaswegian who studied at the School of Art before going to London, first made his name with performance art and with sculpture, both characterized by his particular brand of humour. To those seeking an explanation of his work, the question 'Why?' is usually answered by an irrefutable 'Why not?'

The Modern English paintings in the collection include characteristic works from some of the chief movements of the 20th century.

Vorticism was founded by a group of rebellious artists, led by Wyndham Lewis, who rejected accepted aesthetic norms and are remembered today chiefly for their striking paintings of the Great War. *The dancers* [25] by William Roberts (1895-1980) demonstrates the Vorticist style, in which the figures are faceted into harsh, angular shapes resembling machine parts, and strident colour is used. This composition, along with some abstract wall paintings by Lewis, was carried out as a decoration for an avant-garde London restaurant owner, and shows the debt which the Vorticists owed to Cubism.

23. *William Gear (born 1915)* Summer garden, *1951, canvas 122 × 81.3cm (48 × 32in).*

24. *Bruce McLean (born 1944)* Untitled 1984, *acrylic, chalk and wax on canvas 212.8 × 334cm (83¾ × 131¼in).*

25. *William Roberts (1895-1980)* The dancers, *1919, canvas 152 × 116.5cm (60 × 46in).*

26. *P. Wyndham Lewis (1882-1957)* Froanna, the artist's wife, *1937, canvas 76.2 × 63.5cm (30 × 25in).*

Froanna, the artist's wife [26] by Wyndham Lewis (1882-1957), being a later work, lacks the harsh angularity of the Vorticist period. In this truly stylish portrait, the beauty of the sitter seems to have exercised a powerful influence on the artist.

The most distinguished painter in England during the period 1880-1939 was Walter Sickert (1860-1942) who was friendly with Degas and Whistler and was the father figure of the Camden Town Group (1911-1913) which first introduced Post-Impressionist styles into English art. His scenes of music halls and lower-middle-class life in London were his most influential work. The portrait of the great Cumbrian writer Sir Hugh Walpole [27] dates from his late period, when he sought inspiration in newspaper photographs. Images such as this, which is more an arrangement in tone and colour than a character study, caused puzzlement and much criticism at the time, but can now be seen as an adventurous new departure in English art.

Among the many visionary, even quirky English artists, Stanley Spencer (1891-1959) is one of the most intriguing. At a time when progressive art was concerned with formal and abstract elements, his paintings, so full of narrative content, earned him the title 'individualist'. Among his most successful works are the panels, commissioned by the War Artists' Advisory Commission, of shipyard construction workers, painted between 1940 and 1946 from drawings done at Lithgow's yard, Port Glasgow. Between 1945 and 1950 Spencer also painted a *Resurrection* series of 18 canvases, now dispersed, set in a cemetery in Port Glasgow. *The Glen, Port Glasgow 1952* [30] recalls this series: the children playing on the railings celebrate life after death, while the artist, portfolio under his arm, arrives to record the scene.

The most popularly acclaimed painter of the 20th century in England must surely be L.S. Lowry (1887-1976), who found his subjects in the industrial areas of the north of England. Like the Scottish artist Pringle, for many years he painted quite independently, working in his spare time after office hours, thus evolving a very personal style. *A village square* [28], loosely modelled on a view in Longnor,

Derbyshire, is a typical work in which the almost black figures float around on a milky sea of semi-imaginary industrial streets.

Graham Sutherland (1903-1980), one of the leaders of the English Neo-Romantic School, took his inspiration from shapes in nature, which he saw as mysterious, and often transformed them into near-abstract combinations, as in his renowned *Christ in Majesty* tapestry in Coventry Cathedral. In a painting done for the War Artists' Advisory Commission in 1945 of a bomb depot in France [29], he turned the weird underground rock formations and sinister weapons into a largely two-dimensional composition.

A more analytical approach is evident in the work of Ben Nicholson (1894-1962), doyen of the St Ives School in Cornwall, without doubt the most internationally significant group in England in the middle of this century. In a typical work such as *Still life 1946-50* [31], the painted surface resembles a low-relief sculpture: the objects

27. *Walter R. Sickert (1860-1942)* Sir Hugh Walpole (1884-1941), *1929, canvas 76.2 × 63.5cm (30 × 25in).*

28. *Laurence S. Lowry (1887-1976)* A village square, *1943, canvas 45.7 × 61cm (18 × 24in).*

29. *Graham Sutherland (1903-1980)* Flying bomb depot: the caverns, St Leu d'Esserent 14.1.45., *1945, board 96.5 × 88.9cm (38 × 35in).*

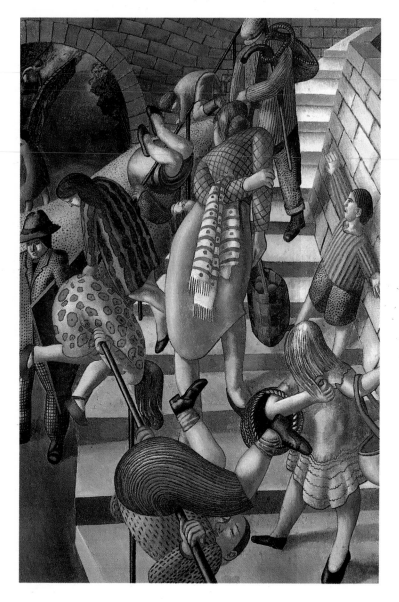

30. *Stanley Spencer (1891-1959)* The Glen, Port Glasgow 1952 *76.2 × 50.9cm (30 × 20in).*

31. *Ben Nicholson (1894-1962)* Still life
1946-1950, *canvas 61 × 50.8cm (24 × 20in).*

32. *Ben Johnson (born 1946)* The keeper,
1977, canvas 205.1 × 134.4cm (81 × 53in).

are indicated simply by outline, and the colour scheme is subdued
and subtle, achieving a quiet, classical sort of balance.

In recent years, abstraction, once held to be the only vehicle for
progressive artists, has been challenged by other fashions, among
them Photorealism. This movement, whose most accomplished
practitioners work in the United States, numbers among its English
disciples Ben Johnson (born 1946), painter of *The keeper* [32], a
striking image of an ice-hockey goalkeeper. The eerie aspect of the
subject, which obviously intrigued the artist, is reinforced by the
monochrome pigment and by the use of airbrushing — a technique
adopted by Photorealists to depersonalize their work by eliminating
the characteristic 'handwriting' of the traditional paintbrush.

Prints and Drawings

The Print Room collection contains over 10,000 prints and 2,500 watercolours and drawings. Because of the innate fragility of works on paper, these are shown only for short periods in the corridor cases outside the picture galleries. The print section includes items by a few old masters but consists mainly of British and European work from the 18th century to the present day, while the majority of the watercolours and drawings are British, of the 19th and 20th centuries.

Of the old masters, Salvator Rosa (1615-1673) is the best represented, with 150 impressions of his etchings. *Jason and the dragon* [1] shows the savagely romantic qualities which made Rosa famous. Jason's swirling pose, as he succeeds in pouring the magic potion over the writhing beast which guards the Golden Fleece, makes a highly charged Baroque composition.

The most exciting prints of the French School are the set of ten woodcuts of Tahitian subjects by Paul Gauguin (1848-1903), which were printed by his son Pola and issued in 1921. *The beautiful land (Navenave fenua)* [2] was done in Brittany in 1894, following the artist's return from his first visit to that South Pacific island paradise during 1891 and 1893. The deliberately rough gouging of the block recalls native art, while the overall blackness of the image is redolent of the demons and spirits which the Tahitians believed to abound, particularly at night.

A group of watercolours by the artists of the Hague School is the highlight of the Dutch section. *The herdswoman* [3] by Anton Mauve (1838-1888) is an example of the simple scenes of the everyday lives of peasants and fisherfolk, which were depicted by the School and

1. *Salvator Rosa (1615-1673)* Jason and the dragon, *c.1664, etching 34 × 21.5cm (13⅜ × 8¼in).*

2. *Paul Gauguin (1848-1903)* The beautiful land (Navenave fenua), *1894, woodcut 35.2 × 20.4cm (14 × 8in).*

3. *Anton Mauve (1838-1888)* The herdswoman, *c.1878, watercolour 24.4 × 33.6cm (9⅝ × 13¼in).*

4. *Charles Rennie Mackintosh (1868-1928)* The village of La Lagonne, *c.1924-1927, watercolour 45.7 × 45.7cm (18 × 18in).*

which found such favour with Scottish collectors and artists, particularly the Glasgow Boys.

As the Print Room was first set up in 1922, at the height of the print collecting boom in Britain, it is natural that the largest and most comprehensive section of the collection is British (particularly Scottish) work of the period from *c.*1880 to 1930. A quartet of Scots who were at the forefront of the etching revival — William Strang, D.Y. Cameron, Muirhead Bone and James McBey (1883-1959) — are well represented. There are impressions of almost all the 751 plates engraved by William Strang (1859-1921) whose *Self portrait no. 6* [8] shows the young artist working on a plate with his etching needle. Strang, a native of Dumbarton, was in great demand as a portraitist but also excelled in genre, illustration and landscape.

D.Y. Cameron (1865-1945) in his early years was associated as a painter with the Glasgow Boys but made his reputation as an etcher. *The Baths of Caracalla* [5], a powerful interpretation of the majestic Roman ruin, is one of his best-known plates and typical of the historic monuments on the Continent which provided much of his inspiration. Cameron also left an impressive legacy of Scottish

5. *David Y. Cameron (1865-1945)* The Baths of Caracalla, *1923, etching and drypoint 27.9 × 43cm (11 × 16⅞in).*

6. *Francis Place (1647-1728)* Dumbarton Castle, c.1701, ink and watercolour *25.2 × 42.4cm (10 × 16⅝in).*

7. *J.M.W. Turner (1775-1851)* Stirling, *c.1831-1834, watercolour 8.9 × 15.5cm (3½ × 6⅛in).*

8. *William Strang (1859-1921)* Self portrait
no. 6, *1885, etching and engraving*
20.2 × 12.6cm (8 × 5in).

views, however, including many of the area around Kippen in the Carse of Stirling, where he lived.

Excellence in watercolour painting is generally held to be one of the outstanding contributions of the English School to the history of art. The school had its beginnings in the work of topographers such as Francis Place (1647-1728), who journeyed north to record *Dumbarton Castle* [6] and other Scottish subjects, using a straightforward outline drawing with watercolour added.

The great J.M.W. Turner (1775-1851) sketched the view of Stirling from Abbey Craig in 1831, when he came to prepare illustrations for works by Sir Walter Scott and stayed with the writer at Abbotsford. The finished watercolour [7], which was executed later, interprets Scott's highly romantic view of Scotland in jewel-like colours and dramatic light effects.

Such was the success of Scott's writings in the 19th century that parts of the Highlands were almost overrun by travellers in search of the historically romantic places and sublime prospects he described. *Loch Coruisk, Skye* [9] by William Daniell (1769-1837) shows an

9. *William Daniell (1769-1837)* Loch Coruisk,
Skye, *c.1815, watercolour 16.2 × 23.7cm*
(6¼ × 9¾in).

10. *Peter de Wint (1784-1849)* A Lincolnshire
landscape, *watercolour 22.2 × 46.8cm*
(8¾ × 18½in).

early group of trippers taking in the awesome grandeur of Scott's 'Coriskin', towered over by the 'peaks of dread' of the rocky Cuillins. This watercolour was painted by Daniell in preparation for one of the most successful aquatint plates in his illustrated books *Voyage round Great Britain,* published between 1814 and 1825.

Most English watercolour artists concentrated more on pastoral scenes, few being more original in outlook than Peter de Wint (1784-1849), who specialized in views around his native Lincolnshire [10]. Economical, freely applied brush strokes epitomize his refreshing style.

A contrast to de Wint is found in the tight style of works by the Pre-Raphaelite Brotherhood, which was perhaps the most significant movement in mid-19th-century English art, and which had several adherents in Scotland. In his *Study from nature, Inverglas* [11] Joseph Noel Paton (1821-1901) shows the meticulous attention to detail that was one of their hallmarks. It bears striking similarities to studies by the artist and critic John Ruskin (1819-1900), who championed the Brotherhood.

Of the Glasgow Boys, two members stand out as supreme masters of the art of watercolour — Arthur Melville (1855-1904) and Joseph Crawhall (1861-1913). Melville's *An eastern harbour* [13], with its broad areas of Chinese white paint offset by splashes of intense colour, is one of the exotic North African subjects for which he became famous. Crawhall, a native of Northumberland, earned his reputation as an animal painter, adopting his own techique of gouache on linen, as in *Horse and cart with lady* [14], a novel composition which owes a debt to Japanese prints. Although hard to believe, it is said that Crawhall painted his animals entirely from memory.

John Quinton Pringle (1864-1925), who has already been noted as a highly inventive oil painter, was also a skilful watercolourist. *Bob* [12], a characteristically intense portrait of a fellow art student, is

11. *Joseph Noel Paton (1821-1901)* Study from nature, Inverglas, *1858, watercolour 38.1 × 53.4cm (15 × 21in).*

12. *John Q. Pringle (1864-1925)* Bob, *1891, watercolour 55 × 34.5cm (22 × 13¾in).*

13. *Arthur Melville (1855-1904)* An eastern harbour, *1894, watercolour 58.5 × 85cm (23 × 33¼in).*

14. *Joseph Crawhall (1861-1913)* Horse and cart with lady, *gouache on linen 22.2 × 29.9cm (8¾ × 11¾in).*

15. *D. Muirhead Bone (1876-1953)* The Court of the Lions, Alhambra, c.*1930-1936, watercolour 37.7 × 27cm (14¾ × 10⅝in).*

16. *Alan Davie (born 1920)* Magic picture no. 45, *1977, gouache 58 × 83cm (23 × 32½in).*

probably his largest, and certainly one of his finest, watercolours and shows his mastery over the medium.

The Glasgow Style practised by architects and interior designers around 1900 and dominated by Charles Rennie Mackintosh (1868-1928) had its parallel in watercolour painting. Mackintosh himself, when his architectural commissions had dried up, devoted the last years of his life to creating brilliant watercolours, many done in the south of France where he lived from 1923. *The village of La Lagonne* [4] shows how he interpreted features of the landscape in almost geometric patterns, his high viewpoint enabling him to create an unusual patchwork effect.

Scottish artists were great travellers, and Muirhead Bone (1876-1953) epitomizes their love of the exotic with his vibrant and detailed *The Court of the Lions, Alhambra* [15], painted to illustrate the lavish book *Old Spain*, which he produced with his sister Gertrude and published in 1936. Bone was also a noted topographer of towns in Britain, an outstanding etcher, and an official war artist in both world wars.

The modern collection as a whole has an emphasis on Scottish art, in which figurative styles prevailed rather longer than elsewhere, but recent trends, from complete abstraction to Photorealism, are also represented in works by some of the best-known international artists. The exotic and unusual are frequently present in the work of Alan Davie (born 1920), a Scottish painter of truly worldwide reputation, who has found inspiration in cultures of all ages, both primitive and sophisticated. His *Magic picture no. 45* [16] is one of a series of images of surprise and mystery, in which he permutates a group of disparate elements, such as a sinister carved mask, the ankh (the Egyptian symbol of divine life), the moon, a wheel (representing eternity), and an aeroplane, which stands for the modern world.

Sculpture

The sculpture collection, numbering around 300 works, covers the period from the late 18th century to the present day and is predominantly of the British School. The late Victorian and Edwardian sections are remarkably strong, a reflection of the era of commercial affluence which brought sculptors from all over the country to Glasgow to decorate the many imposing buildings being erected in the city at that time. A select group of French sculptures has been acquired over the years to complement the better-known paintings of that school, while the collection of work by contemporary sculptors is gradually increasing.

A variety of different materials and methods of production is represented. In casting processes, of course, it is usually the case that the resulting work in plaster, bronze or even terracotta is not unique but is one of an edition, while the use of the pointing machine, particularly prevalent in the 19th century, allowed works carved in stone or wood to be repeated, scaled up or reduced, in the sculptor's workshop. As a result, many pieces of sculpture are, like prints, duplicated in several collections.

British School
It would be hard to justify any strong tradition of British sculpture before the end of the 18th century — the dominant figures until then had been artists from abroad, especially those from the Low Countries, such as Rysbrack, Roubiliac and Scheemakers — but with the founding of the Royal Academy in 1768 and the advent of the classical revival, home-grown talent came to the fore to satisfy the increasing taste for portraits and statuary.

There is no more splendid portrait in the collection than the statue of *William Pitt* [1] by John Flaxman (1755-1826), commissioned by the citizens of Glasgow to be placed in the old Town Hall in 1812. Flaxman's antique-style reliefs, designed for use on the famous Wedgwood pottery, stamped him as one of the leaders of the Neoclassical movement. Pitt, although dressed in contemporary clothes, is shown in a pose derived from Greek and Roman statuary, which gives him an air of authority appropriate to the character of a great parliamentarian.

In the more expressive bust of *James Watt* [2], Flaxman's contemporary Francis Chantrey (1781-1841) shows his mastery over white marble, the preferred medium of the Neoclassicists. The loose drapery, modelled on the Roman toga, was a standard feature of portraits of the period, but Chantrey, through his ability to show character in the thoughtfully resigned expression of the old engineer and inventor, imparts to the work an ageless quality.

The figure group was another area which occupied sculptors in the 19th century. Classically inspired subjects gradually gave way to the 'fancy piece' whose theme was taken from more recent literature, history, or everyday life. An example is *Motherless* [4] by George Lawson (1832-1904) which dates from the High Victorian period and

1. *John Flaxman (1755-1826)* William Pitt 1759-1806, *1812, marble, height 192.3cm (76in).*

2. *Francis Chantrey (1781-1841)* James Watt 1736-1819, *1816, marble, height 55cm (21¼in).*

3. *E. Roscoe Mullins (1848-1907)* Isaac and Esau *(detail), 1904, marble, 118 × 227 × 108cm (46¼ × 89¼ × 42¼in).*

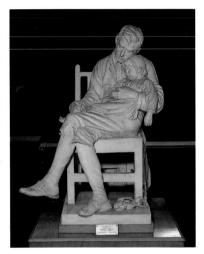

4. *George Lawson (1832-1904)* Motherless, *c.1889, plaster, height 135cm (53¼in).*

5. *W. Goscombe John (1860-1952)* The elf, *1899, marble, height 104cm (41in) displayed in Kibble Palace, Botanic Gardens, Glasgow.*

possesses the strong anecdotal features and emotional quality of the art of that era. A firm favourite with succeeding generations of Gallery visitors, this is probably the only piece by which Lawson is generally known.

As a reaction to the emotional excesses of some Victorian sculptors and to the jaded, watered-down Neoclassicism of others, there arose in England in the 1880s a movement known as the New Sculpture which breathed fresh life into the art. Leading figures in the movement, such as Alfred Gilbert, George Frampton, Alfred Drury, Harry Bates and Derwent Wood, who are all represented in this, the strongest section of the Gallery collection, sought inspiration in the work of Renaissance sculptors like Donatello and Michelangelo and sometimes added an element of mysterious symbolism all their own. Another key feature, the enlivening of the surface texture, is evident in the massive marble by E. Roscoe Mullins (1848-1907) of the Old Testament story of *Isaac and Esau* [3]; it illustrates the crucial moment when the elder son pleads with his blind father for the birthright denied him by his brother Jacob. This intensely dramatic subject, which has the alternative title *Bless me, even me also, O my Father,* is powerfully portrayed.

The mysterious aspect of the New Sculpture is represented by the alluring carving of *The elf* [5] by the Welsh sculptor Goscombe John (1860-1952). The interest in Celtic mythology which was typical of the period is apparent in the title and in the carved pattern on the base. This piece is typical of the whimsical nature of much of the sculpture and painting produced in the 1890s.

Pittendrigh Macgillivray (1856-1938), painter, poet, pamphleteer, and the only sculptor member of the Glasgow Boys, is not usually classed as a New Sculptor, but he certainly adopted their style. His heroic bronze bust *Thenew, mother of St Kentigern* [6] again illustrates the Celtic past. The 6th-century legend of Thenew, also known as Enoch, tells how she was cast adrift in the sea by her half-pagan father but survived to give birth to Kentigern, who is better known as St Mungo, patron saint of the City of Glasgow.

The most prominent 20th-century Scottish sculptor after Macgillivray was Benno Schotz (1891-1984), who was born in Estonia but settled in Glasgow in 1912. Although he executed figure compositions, religious sculptures and even some semi-abstract work, he is best known for his modelled portraits, most of which were cast in bronze. The terracotta *Self portrait* [7] shows his vigorous and direct style.

The Gallery is expanding its 20th-century collection and has a few significant works by important exponents of non-figurative styles. Eduardo Paolozzi, born in Leith in 1924 of Italian parents, now lives in London and Germany and is a major international figure. *Hamlet in a Japanese manner* [8] is a purely abstract work constructed in 1966 at the height of the Pop Art movement of which he was one of the chief protagonists. Paolozzi has for long had a fixation with the machine, and this piece was welded together from aluminium castings and material from engineering works. The artist originally painted *Hamlet* in striking colours which he later removed. The puzzling title was chosen to underline the shock and confusion caused by the bold, challenging nature of the work.

Anthony Caro (born 1924) is an English sculptor of international acclaim working in an abstract idiom. *Table piece Z85* [11] which has the provocative subtitle *Tiptoe*, is a work without any hidden meaning, the sculptor having merely striven to create a visually stimulating and enjoyable combination of shapes, with some textural interest being added by the pitted and rusted metal surface.

6. *J. Pittendrigh Macgillivray (1856-1938)* Thenew, mother of St Kentigern, *1915, bronze, height 59cm (23¼in).*

7. *Benno Schotz (1891-1984)* Self portrait, *1953, terracotta, height 51.7cm (20⅜in).*

8. *Eduardo Paolozzi (born 1924)* Hamlet in a Japanese manner, *1966, three-part aluminium construction, 165 × 343 × 155cm (65 × 135 × 61in).*

9. *Jean-Antoine Houdon (1741-1828)* Georges Louis Leclerc, Count de Buffon, *1781, tinted plaster, height 61cm (24in).*

10. *Jean-Baptiste Carpeaux (1827-1875)* Susanna surprised, *1872, terracotta, height 63.5cm (25in).*

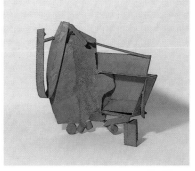

11. *Anthony Caro (born 1924)* Table piece Z 85 — tiptoe, *1982, welded steel, 87.5 × 107 × 76.2cm (34½ × 42¼ × 30in).*

12. *Ossip Zadkine (1890-1967)* The music group, *1926, bronze, height 57cm (22½in).*

French School

The collection of French sculpture which is displayed in the Gallery alongside the paintings of that school contains some fine bronzes by Degas, Rodin and Renoir. Among the less familiar items is the tinted plaster bust of *Georges Louis Leclerc, Count de Buffon* [9] by Jean-Antoine Houdon (1741-1828), one of the outstanding European sculptors of his day. This direct yet subtle portrait of the eminent natural historian was commissioned by Queen Catherine II of Russia. Houdon's very personal style is based on a close study of detail, and in it may be discerned the lively movement found in the work of the Baroque sculptor Bernini combined with the dignity of ancient Roman art.

Jean-Baptiste Carpeaux (1827-1875) was one of the French sculptors whose work inspired the New Sculpture in England. His *Susanna surprised* [10] ripples with movement, emphasizing the panic in the young woman's face when she realizes the Elders are watching her bathe. Carpeaux enjoyed great success, especially for his lively carving of the sculpture group *La Danse,* carried out for the Paris Opéra in 1869.

Unlike some movements in painting, such as Impressionism, Cubism finds equally valid expression in sculpture. The simplification of shape and form in *The music group* [12] by Ossip Zadkine (1890-1967) is familiar to students of Picasso and Braque, and this sculpture dates from the height of the Cubist movement. Zadkine was born in Russia, but after studying in London moved in 1909 to Paris, which, with the recent birth of Cubism, was emerging at that time as the centre for the development of the most important movements in modern art.

Branch Museums

The steady growth of Glasgow's rich and varied collections has necessitated the finding of buildings to house them. The Department of Museums and Art Galleries is made up at present of nine separate buildings — the Art Gallery and Museum, Kelvingrove; the People's Palace; the Burrell Collection; the Museum of Transport; Pollok House; Haggs Castle; Camphill House; Provand's Lordship and Rutherglen Museum. Each has its own emphasis and personality.

All the branch museums, with the exception of the People's Palace which opened in 1898, have been created within the last 25 years: the Museum of Transport in Albert Drive in 1964; Pollok House in 1967; Haggs Castle in 1976; Rutherglen Museum in 1981; and the Burrell Collection and Provand's Lordship in 1983. Between 1979 and 1982 exhibitions were mounted at St Enoch's Exhibition Centre and it is hoped that a similar downtown gallery may be available in the future.

This growth has brought about a greater support and interest from people both at home and abroad and the efforts of the staff to expand displays of collections acquired over the years has succeeded in making the museums more popular. A very great proportion of these collections was donated but recently the number of items acquired by purchase has increased. This does not mean that our purchase fund has increased — quite the reverse — but emphasis has been given to the buying of specimens of a less expensive nature, such as Scottish arts, crafts and natural history, with a number of fine examples of fine and decorative arts, ethnographical material, together with technological and arms and armour specimens to fill gaps in our otherwise comprehensive collections.

The People's Palace
Opened in 1898 to encourage interest in the arts amongst working people, it stands on historic Glasgow Green. It is a museum of the social and political history of Glasgow and its environs and today enjoys well-deserved support from a growing number of visitors.

Exterior view of the People's Palace, Glasgow Green.

Burrell Collection

Gifted to the city in 1944 by Sir William and Lady Burrell, this remarkable collection of medieval stained glass, furniture and tapestries, Chinese and Near Eastern ceramics, French Impressionist paintings and objects from the ancient civilizations is housed in a purpose-built museum in Pollok Park which makes a splendid setting for such a collection.

View of the Medieval Gallery of the Burrell Collection.

The main entrance to the Burrell Collection with the gallery beyond.

Museum of Transport

Glasgow's history of shipbuilding, railway locomotive building and car manufacture made it inevitable that there should be such a museum, but it was not opened until 1964. Displays include tramcars, carriages, bicycles, railway engines, motor cars, buses and a magnificent collection of model ships, some of which had formerly been on view at Kelvingrove House. Preparations are well under way for the removal of the collections to the newly refurbished Kelvin Hall which will house both a sports complex and the enlarged museum.

An Arrol-Johnston car of 1906 from the Museum of Transport, photographed in Pollok Park.

A Royal Mail carriage from the Museum of Transport photographed in the grounds of Pollok House.

Pollok House

Built between 1748 and 1752 this handsome Palladian house was the home of the Maxwells of Pollok until it was presented to the City in 1966. It houses part of the splendid collection of Spanish paintings acquired by Sir William Stirling Maxwell in the middle of the 19th century, together with furniture, ceramics, glass and silver as well as other paintings, including important works by William Blake.

Pollok House and its garden.

Pollok House and the River Cart.

Haggs Castle

Opened in 1976 with the object of interesting children in the way of life of the past, particularly the 16th century, it is housed in a much restored castle originally built between 1585 and 1587 by John Maxwell (who became 12th of Pollok).

Part of the collection of Victorian toys at Haggs Castle.

Exterior view of Haggs Castle.

Provand's Lordship

The oldest domestic building left in Glasgow, dating from 1471, this small but attractive museum displays medieval furniture in period room settings and material from the more recent past including the Morton sweet shop.

An interior view of Provand's Lordship.

Part of the collections at Rutherglen Museum.

Rutherglen Museum

A small museum of the history of this ancient Royal burgh, joined to Glasgow in the reorganization of local government in 1975, housed in the former burgh court building.

Camphill House

Camphill House was built around 1818 for Robert Thomson, the textile manufacturer, whose son Neale later sold to the city the land which was to become Queen's Park. It currently houses the extensive costume and textile collections which may be visited by appointment only.

Three Victorian dresses from the collection at Camphill House.

Gallery Plan

Ground Floor

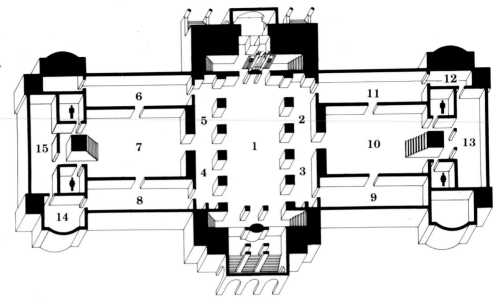

1 Centre Hall	**6** Archaeology	**11** Ethnography
2 Exhibition Area	**7** Arms and Armour	**12** Biology
3 Enquiries Desk	**8** Exhibition Gallery	**13** Birdlife
4 Gallery Shop	**9** Geology	**14** Lecture Room
5 Coffee Shop	**10** Natural History of Scotland	**15** Glasgow Style

First Floor

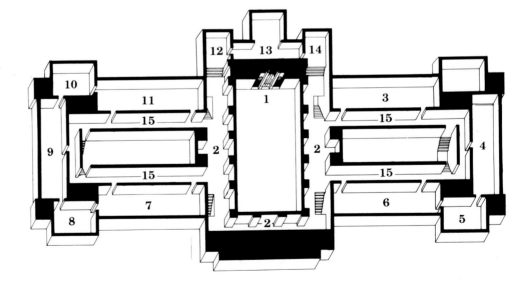

1 Organ	**6** British Painting: Gallery IV	**11** French Painting
2 Decorative Art	**7** Italian Painting	**12** Glass
3 British Painting: Gallery I	**8** Flemish Painting	**13** Tea Room
4 British Painting: Gallery II	**9** Dutch Painting	**14** Silver
5 British Painting: Gallery III	**10** French Painting	**15** Exhibition Areas

Index

Figures in italic denote illustrations